Wo

Other Standard Ic

 Run a macro

Turn STEP and TRACE mode on

Insert columns

Insert a sheet

Start the Solver

Select the cell to reference or link to

Delete selected rows

Delete selected sheets

Choose SmartIcons

Insert rows

Delete selected columns

Graph Window Icons

Current Palette (Default)

Draw an arrow

Draw a line

Draw an ellipse

Draw a polygon

Draw a rectangle

Add text

Draw freehand

Line graph

Vertical bar graph

Horizontal bar graph

Mixed graph

Pie chart

Area graph

HLCO (High/Low/Close/Open) graph

3D line graph

3D bar graph

3D pie chart

3D area graph

Select a graph type

Delete permanently

Duplicate

Rotate 90 degrees

Flip horizontal

Flip vertical

Move object in front

Move object in back

Others: Cascade, Copy object, Enlarge, Reduce, Rotate continuously, Tile, XY graph, and Zoom.

SYBEX

Lotus 1-2-3® for Windows™ Instant Reference

Gerald E. Jones

SYBEX®

San Francisco • Paris • Düsseldorf • Soest

Acquisitions Editor: David Clark
Developmental Editor: James A. Compton
Copy Editor: Janna Hecker Clark
Technical Editor: Sheldon M. Dunn
Production Editor: Carolina Montilla
Word Processors: Ann Dunn, Susan Trybull
Series Designer and Production Artist: Ingrid Owen
Technical Art: Delia Brown
Screen Graphics: Cuong Le
Desktop Publishing Production: Len Gilbert
Proofreaders: Lisa Haden, Dina F. Quan
Indexer: Ted Laux
Cover Designer: Archer Design

Library of Congress Card Number: 91-66348
ISBN: 0-89588-864-5

Manufactured in the United States of America
10 9 8 7 6 5 4 3 2

Acknowledgments

A team of dedicated professionals worked to develop and produce this book. At SYBEX, thanks to David Clark, Acquisitions Editor; James A. Compton, Instant Reference Series Editor; Janna Hecker Clark, Editor; and Sheldon M. Dunn, Technical Editor. Thanks also to Kimberly Twist at Lotus Development Corporation for furnishing software. Special thanks are due William Ditto of Bell Computer Systems for providing a 386SX/25 computer system for software testing. And a personal thank you to Georja Jones for keeping the faith through some challenging deadlines.

Table of Contents

Introduction

Part One

Windows and 1-2-3

Part Two

The Main Menu

Part Three

The Graph Window Menu

Part Four

@Functions

Appendix A

SmartIcons

Appendix B

The Translate Utility

Appendix C

Macro Language

Introduction

The idea governing this book is a simple one. When you are thwarted by a function or procedure in Lotus 1-2-3 for Windows, or require a quick refresher on spreadsheet techniques, you want a single source of information to solve your problems quickly. This book, which covers Lotus 1-2-3 for Windows through Release 1.0a, is intended to meet those needs.

Lotus 1-2-3 for Windows Instant Reference will provide the information essential to getting the most from this powerful version of 1-2-3. The book covers basic spreadsheet analysis and output operations, as well as functions, macros, graphing, and built-in desktop publishing features. Features that will be new to users of Releases 2 and 3 are summarized in the "For Experienced Users of 1-2-3" section of this introduction.

Because we expect you to consult this book as a reference for solving day-to-day application problems, we have assumed that your copy of the program is already installed. Some installation notes will be found in Part I in the entries "Install 1-2-3" and "Memory Usage." To customize the program once installation has been performed, see "File Page Setup," "File Printer Setup," "Tools User Setup," and "Worksheet Global Settings" in Part II.

A QUICK INTRODUCTION TO 1-2-3 FOR WINDOWS

The following notes cover some of the questions commonly encountered when installing and running Lotus 1-2-3 for Windows. You must install Windows first, then 1-2-3.

To Start the Program:

1. Load Microsoft Windows. At the DOS prompt, key in **win**. (If you intend to work in Windows regularly, this instruction should be added to the AUTOEXEC.BAT file so that Windows loads automatically when you boot your computer.)

2. The Program Manager window should be displayed. If it is not open, select the **Program Manager** icon.
3. In the Program Manager window, double-click on the **Lotus Applications** icon, or press **Alt-W** and select its item number.
4. In the Lotus Applications window, double-click on the **1-2-3 for Windows** icon, or move to it with the arrow keys and press ↵.
5. An hourglass icon appears at the pointer location, indicating that you must wait for the program to load. The 1-2-3 for Windows application window appears. When the pointer changes from an hourglass to an arrow and when READY is displayed in the top right corner of the screen, the program is ready for your input.

For more information on Windows and opening a worksheet in 1-2-3, see Part I.

For Experienced Users of 1-2-3

If you are an experienced user of Lotus 1-2-3, you can begin using the Windows version immediately, if necessary. When you see the Main Menu displayed across the top of the screen, simply press the slash (/) key, just as you have always done to initiate commands. (You can also press the less-than (<) symbol.) Pressing either of these keys brings up the 1-2-3 Classic menu, which contains the commands that are familiar to you. You can continue by pressing the first letter of the menu item you wish to select, then pressing the first letter of each submenu, and finally entering any options. In short, you can use the Classic menu as you did in previous releases of 1-2-3. *Note that the command set corresponds to Lotus 1-2-3 Release 3.1.*

Similarly, you can press the colon (:) key to work with the WYSIWYG menu. Keep in mind, however, that your productivity should increase and you can use much more extensive capabilities if you learn to work in the Windows environment. To do this, you need to use the 1-2-3 Main Menu. (For more information, see "The Classic Menu" in Part I.)

Users of Release 3.1 will find that some capabilities have simply been redesigned to suit the Windows environment, while others will be new. Users familiar with Releases 2.01 and 2.2 will find the following new features in the Windows version:

Accelerator keys The selection of accelerator keys (for quickly bypassing menu selections) has been expanded. The Alt key activates the 1-2-3 Main Menu, just as the slash (/) or less-than (<) keys activate the Classic menu.

Classic menu Optionally, you can use traditional 1-2-3 keystroke commands. However, bear in mind that some of the commands no longer apply and do not operate.

Copy This command has been renamed. (To copy data from a range, see "Edit Quick Copy.")

Data Menu items have been added for additional what-if tables, as well as connection to tables in external databases. Through a new feature called DataLens, you can access dBASE, SQL, and Paradox data tables, which can reside on a PC disk, CD-ROM device, network server, or mainframe. New database commands are Data Connect to External and Data External Options. The Data Table command (in Releases 2.*x*) has been renamed Data What-if Table, and can be defined as 1-, 2-, or 3-way (using one formula and as many as three variables). (See Part II.)

Edit The Release 2.*x* commands Copy, Move, Range Erase, and Range Search have been changed. Some new Edit menu items make use of the Windows features of the Clipboard (scratch-pad memory area) and Dynamic Data Exchange (DDE, data transfer with concurrent Windows application programs). New commands include Edit Clear (instead of Range Erase), Edit Clear Special, Edit Find (instead of Range Search), Edit Move Cells (instead of Move), Edit Quick Copy (instead of Copy), and Edit Undo.

File New options are available for network file protection and file printing. New commands include File Open (instead of File Retrieve), File Exit (instead of File Quit), and File Save As (rename). Instead of the Print command, 1-2-3 for Windows uses the printer control commands File Page Setup, File Preview, File Print, and File Printer Setup.

Function keys The set of available function keys has been expanded.

@Functions The available @functions, or predefined formulas, have been expanded. (See Part IV.)

Graph Capabilities for generating charts and graphs, as well as annotations and drawings, have been expanded through a new Graph menu.

Help The new on-line help facility extends the Windows system of icons, indexes, and list boxes. (See "Help" in Part I.)

Macros The macro programming language has been expanded, with new debugging tools. (See Appendix C.)

Move This command has been renamed. (See "Edit Move Cells.")

Print Instead of the former Print command, menu items for printing operations will be found on the File menu.

Range Ranges can be selected either before or after initiating a command. Three-dimensional ranges can also be specified.

Style Graphic capabilities for spreadsheet publishing have been added, including integration of Adobe Type Manager (ATM). You now have control of colors, fonts, label alignment, shading, and range borders. (For more information on ATM, which is bundled with the program, see Appendix D.)

Tools More user settings are available. What-if analysis with Backsolver and Solver utilities has been enhanced. (Add-in programs, if used, must be Windows versions.)

Window This selection on the Main Menu permits you to manipulate 1-2-3 menus as display windows, and includes the cascade, split, and tile windows features.

Worksheet Rows and columns can now be sized with the mouse, and there is a new command Worksheet Row Height. Cell formats and settings can be assigned to all worksheets in the current file through Worksheet Global Group. Multiple-sheet files are supported.

File Compatibility

The data file structure of 1-2-3 is the same as that of Release 3 and has .WK3 (worksheet) and .FM3 (format) extensions. Files with these extensions are therefore interchangeable between the Windows and Release 3 versions. However, if you add graphic effects such as special fonts and colors in Windows, these enhancements may not be accessible if you subsequently read the file with the Release 3 program. For information about working with worksheet files of prior 1-2-3 releases, see Appendix B, "The Translate Utility."

Prior Versions and Excel The 1-2-3 for Windows program can read the following file formats without translation: .WK1, .ALL, .FMT. The program can *read* data files from all previous versions of 1-2-3, data files of Allways and Symphony, as well as Microsoft Excel .XLS files. The program can *read and write* the .WK1 files of 1-2-3 Release 2.

Optionally, you can choose to save a file in .WK1 format. Any file having the same name with that extension will be overwritten. *Be aware that some data and formatting may be lost or damaged when saving a .WK3 worksheet as a .WK1 file.* A warning message to this effect will appear when you try to save the file. In particular, all Windows-related settings will be lost. Multisheet files cannot be saved in this format.

OS/2 Files The 1-2-3 program cannot work directly with the data files generated by 1-2-3/G (releases that run under the OS/2 operating system).

Translate Utility You can translate .WK3 files into other formats with the embedded Translate utility. (See Appendix B.)

Macro Compatibility Release 3.1 macros that rely entirely on keystrokes can be run in 1-2-3 for Windows through the Classic menu. Macro calls to commands that no longer operate in this version are ignored.

Macros created in Release 2 or 3 can be used with 1-2-3 for Windows but may have to be edited by substituting revised command names. (Consult the "Command Cross-Reference" table in the *1-2-3 User's Guide.*)

To use a macro created in Release 2, first load the corresponding .WK1 file into 1-2-3 for Windows. Use the **Macro Library Manager Load** command in Release 2 to retrieve a macro from a library, edit the macro and worksheet in that program, and then save the edited worksheet as a .WK1 file before loading it into 1-2-3 for Windows.

You can also use edited Release 2 macros with .WK3 files. To use the macros with only one .WK3 file, load both the .WK1 file containing the macros and the .WK3 file into 1-2-3 for Windows and then use the **Edit Quick Copy** command to copy the macros to the new file.

To use Release 2 macros with multiple .WK3 files, you must follow the procedure described above to copy the macros to a .WK3 macro library file (a worksheet that contains only macros), then load that file into 1-2-3 for Windows along with the other .WK3 data files.

LAN Installation The 1-2-3 for Windows program can be installed on a network server if you begin with the Install disk (Disk 1 in the distribution set). To install Adobe Type Manager (ATM) as well, you must have write access to the subdirectory WINDOWS\SYSTEM. Once the program has been installed on the server, installation to any node can be performed by selecting the Install 1-2-3 icon. However, you cannot install to another server by selecting this icon.

Controls

The Mouse In the Windows version, menu selections are made and option settings are chosen with a pointing device, such as a mouse, and data are input mainly through the keyboard. Using the Graph capabilities (especially drawing) will be cumbersome without some type of pointing device.

The program assumes a single-button input device, such as the Microsoft Mouse. If you have a mouse with two or three buttons, only the leftmost button is used. However, the right button has some uses with Graph features and SmartIcons. (For more information about using a mouse with Windows and 1-2-3 for Windows, see "The Mouse" in Part I.)

Instructions in this book call for three types of actions with the mouse:

Click Move the pointer with the mouse to the item described in the instruction and press the mouse button briefly, once.

Double-click Move the pointer with the mouse to the item described in the instruction and press the mouse button twice in rapid succession.

Drag Press the mouse button, hold it down while moving the pointer to the desired position, and then release the button.

Submenus If you see an arrowhead (➤) after the name of an item in a pull-down menu, selecting that item will cause a submenu to appear. In Windows terminology, this submenu is called a *cascading menu*, or *cascade*.

If you see an ellipsis (...) after the name of an item in a pull-down menu, selecting that item will cause a *dialog box* to appear. A dialog box is a special window display in which you can change option settings.

Options In general, options are set within dialog boxes. In Windows, different kinds of graphic symbols are used within dialog boxes to indicate the type of selection being made. (For more information about the controls in dialog boxes, see "Menus" in Part I.)

Windows In the Windows environment, framed areas of the screen can represent different programs and files. A program window is called an *application*, and a file window is called a *document*. Multiple windows can be open at the same time, as when working on multiple-sheet 1-2-3 files or when doing some type of multitasking, such as editing a worksheet while printing a document with a word processing program.

For more information about controlling windows, either with the mouse or through the keyboard, see "Windows" in Part I.

HOW TO USE THIS INSTANT REFERENCE

For ease of use, this Instant Reference is divided into the following sections:

Introduction This section covers background information on Lotus 1-2-3 for Windows and gives directions for using this book.

Part I: Windows and 1-2-3 Entries in this section correspond to features of the Windows environment that help you get around in 1-2-3, including use of the Classic menu, mouse, keyboard, menus, windows, and on-line help.

Part II: The Main Menu When you are making entries into a worksheet, the Main Menu, a selection of pull-down menus, is displayed at the top of the 1-2-3 program window. (The Main Menu is also called the Worksheet menu.) Entries in this section of the book correspond to the items in each of these pull-down menus, and are listed alphabetically. Omitted from this part of the book are the Graph menu (covered in Part III) and the Help menu (covered in Part I).

Part III: The Graph Window Menu The Graph pull-down from the Main Menu presents its own control bar of pull-downs. It is so extensive in its capabilities that it is covered separately here. Entries correspond to the items in each of its pull-down menus, and are listed alphabetically.

Part IV: @Functions Predefined formulas, or @functions, are covered in this part. Entries are arranged alphabetically within the following groups: database, data and time, financial, logical, mathematical, special, statistical, and string functions.

Appendix A: SmartIcons A row of icons normally appears in the program window. You can click on an icon as a shortcut to selecting some of the commands. A separate group of icons is available when you are working in the Graph menu. Consult this appendix and the inside front covers for icons and their corresponding actions.

Appendix B: The Translate Utility An embedded program for converting worksheet files to and from other formats is described in this appendix.

Appendix C: Macro Language Macros can be recorded interactively or can be written in macro command language. Each macro command is listed here with a brief summary.

Appendix D: Adobe Type Manager This program is bundled with 1-2-3 for Windows for the purpose of generating sharper displays, as well as presentation-quality typography in outputs. Notes cover installation and use of this program.

Endpapers SmartIcons and their definitions are shown on the inside front cover of this book. On the inside back cover are listings of the function, accelerator, and navigation keys.

Procedures

Each entry in this book is designed to provide the information essential to understanding a particular feature of 1-2-3 for Windows in a clear, accessible format. When you need to be reminded only of the menu sequence to follow, see the entry's "To..." section.

While all actions in the Windows version can be handled through the keyboard, if necessary, the discussion in this book assumes that you are using a keyboard *and* a mouse. The instructions in this book refer first to the mouse actions required for menu selections and option settings with a minimum of keyboarding. However, for situations in which you might be using only the keyboard, as in data entry operations, the required keystrokes are given.

Following Instruction Steps To show at a glance the alternative paths you can follow in a single menu sequence, the instructions in this book specify the item to be selected at each step. Because the emphasis is on using the mouse to make menu selections, not all methods will necessarily be shown. A typical sequence of steps looks like this:

To Set Printer Options:

1. From the Main Menu, select **File.**
2. From the File pull-down, select **Printer Setup.**

3. In the File Printer Setup dialog box, select the printer name in the Printer list box.
4. To accept the default options for the printer you've selected, select the **OK** button.
   or
   To change the options, select the **Setup** button.
5. A dialog box containing options for the installed printer appears. Reset the options shown. (See "Options," below.)
6. Select **OK**.

Notes, Options, and Cross-References Exceptions and possible pitfalls are described under the "Notes" headings. These sections also may include suggestions as to the most efficient work method when several alternatives are available.

The next section of longer entries is headed "Options" and usually covers any settings that can be made in submenus and dialog boxes.

Finally, where appropriate, you'll find cross-references to features of related interest under the heading "See Also."

Part One

Windows and 1-2-3

This portion of the book covers features of the Microsoft Windows operating environment, as well as techniques for controlling menus and document windows within 1-2-3 for Windows. You will want to refer to these entries particularly if you are already familiar with Release 2 or 3 of Lotus 1-2-3 but are just becoming acquainted with Windows.

THE CLASSIC MENU

Key commands used in 1-2-3 Release 3.1 can be entered directly into the Windows version through the Classic menu (Figure I.1).

To Use the Classic Menu:

1. When the Main Menu is displayed and the READY mode indicator is visible in the top right corner of the screen, press either the **slash** (/) or **less-than** (<) key.
   or
   Press the **colon** (:) key to enter Release 3.1 WYSIWYG commands.
2. The 1-2-3 Classic menu appears at the top of the screen. Press the key corresponding to the first letter of the command you wish to execute.
   or
   Press → or ← to move the highlight to the desired command, then press ↵ to select it.
3. The submenu for the command you selected appears. Repeat step 2 to select the desired command from the submenu.
4. Repeat step 2 for each submenu that appears.
5. Enter cell addresses, ranges, or data as prompted by the program to complete the command, then press ↵.
   or
   To return to the worksheet before a command is executed, thus turning off the Classic menu, press **Esc**.

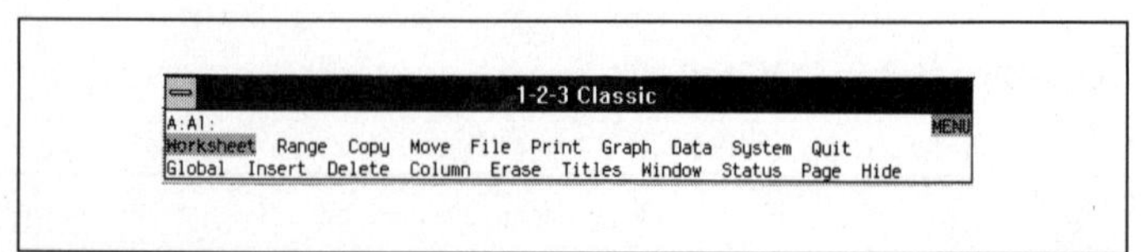

Figure I.1: The 1-2-3 Classic Menu

• **NOTES** Some Release 3.1 commands included on the menu no longer operate in the same way because of differences in the Windows version. Release 3.1 commands that are *obsolete* in 1-2-3 for Windows include:

/Worksheet Global Default Other Clock Clock

/Worksheet Global Default Other Clock Filename

/Worksheet Global Default Other Help Instant

/Worksheet Global Default Other Help Removable

/Worksheet Global Default Status

/Worksheet Global Default Temp

/Worksheet Status

/Worksheet Window Display

:Display Font-Directory

:Display Options Intensity

:Display Rows

:Graph View

To use Add-ins with the Classic menu, press **Alt-F10.** To escape from the Classic menu, press **Esc** repeatedly, press **Ctrl-Break,** or press **Alt-F4.**

THE CLIPBOARD

In the Windows environment, the *Clipboard* is a scratch-pad memory area through which you can pass data to other programs and documents that are currently active and open.

To Use the Clipboard:

1. In Windows, start the application that holds the source data.
2. Select the data to be passed to the Clipboard.
3. Select either **Copy** or **Cut** from the application's Edit menu.

4. The data are now on the Clipboard. You can exit or minimize the current application, if you wish.
5. During the same work session and before you use Edit Cut or Edit Copy again, start the application that will receive the data from the Clipboard.
6. Open the document that will receive the data and move the pointer to the place where the insertion should appear.
7. Select **Paste** from the application's Edit menu.
8. The data appear at the specified place in the open document.

• NOTES This procedure applies to most Windows applications, including 1-2-3 for Windows. See the *Microsoft Windows User's Guide* for information on passing data to non-Windows applications, which can only be done in 386 enhanced mode.

In step 7, the Paste operation can be performed repeatedly to retrieve multiple copies of the same data. If you wish, this data can be copied into multiple documents and applications. The contents of the Clipboard do not change until you perform Edit Cut or Edit Copy again, or until you end the Windows work session.

To perform Dynamic Data Exchange (DDE) between a Windows application and 1-2-3 for Windows, see "Edit Link Options" in Part II.

• OPTIONS In step 5, select **Cut** to remove the data from the current document and move it to the Clipboard. Select **Copy** to retain the data in the current document and place another copy of it on the Clipboard.

See Also Part II: *Edit Copy, Edit Cut, Edit Link Options, Edit Paste.*

THE CONTROL MENU

The small bar in the box in the top left corner of the current window is the access point to the Control menu for that window (Figure I.2).

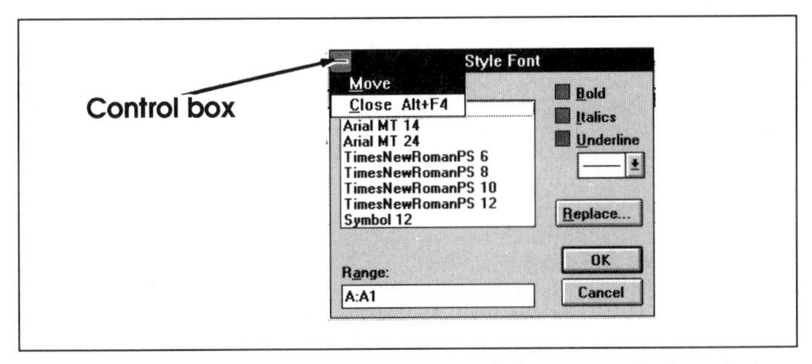

Figure I.2: The Control box is in the top left corner of any window

To Gain Control of an Open Window:

1. Click on the window's Control box.
   or
   If the window is the 1-2-3 application window itself or any dialog box, press **Alt-spacebar.** For any other window within 1-2-3, press **Alt-hyphen.**
2. The Control menu appears. Make a selection by clicking on the item, pressing its underscored letter, or pressing the accelerator key listed to the right of the item.

• NOTES In the Windows environment, windows are of two types: application (task, or program) and document. In 1-2-3, worksheets are displayed in document windows.

Since the program supports three-dimensional worksheets, multiple document windows may be open on the desktop (screen) concurrently. Use the **Next** command in the Control menu to move among worksheets.

• OPTIONS Options in the Control menu for any window can include the following: (Dimmed items are not available to you at this point in the program.)

Restore After a window has been maximized (enlarged) or minimized (shrunk), restores it to its former size.

Move Lets you move the window to another location on the desktop (screen) by using the arrow keys or dragging the title bar to a new location with the mouse.

Size Lets you change the size of a window by using the arrow keys or by dragging an edge or corner to a new location with the mouse. Dialog boxes cannot be resized.

Minimize Shrinks the window to an icon.

Maximize Enlarges the window to the largest size at which it can be displayed on the screen.

Close Terminates the running of the window's task or closes the file it represents. The accelerator key for this command is Ctrl-F4.

Next When multiple document windows are displayed, switches to the next open document. The accelerator key for this command is Ctrl-F6.

Paste In Real and Standard modes only, lets you copy text from the Clipboard, or scratch-pad memory area of Windows, into a document window.

Edit, Settings Appear only on Windows Control menus. These apply to non-Windows applications in 386 mode and are not available with 1-2-3. The Edit command displays a cascading menu of Clipboard operations, and Settings controls multitasking. Use them when running other applications, such as database programs, concurrently with 1-2-3 for Windows.

Switch To Lets you change to a different application by using the Windows Task List (a listing of currently running programs). The accelerator key for this command is Ctrl-Esc.

See Also *Minimize/Maximize, Windows.*

INSTALL 1-2-3

This program handles all the details of transferring 1-2-3 and related files from the distribution disks to your computer system. Once installation has been performed, the 1-2-3 Install icon appears in the Lotus Applications window and can be selected for modifying system parameters and other maintenance operations.

To Install 1-2-3 for Windows:

1. Insert the distribution disk marked *Install* in drive A of your computer.
2. Start Windows by entering **win** at the DOS prompt.
3. If the Program Manager window does not appear, open it by double-clicking on the **Program Manager** icon.
4. Select **File**.
5. From the File menu, select **Run**.
6. In the Command Line text box in the Run window, enter **a:install.exe**.
7. Select the **OK** button.
8. When the introductory screen of Install appears, select the **OK** button to start the installation.
9. As Install presents each dialog box to you, make the selections, enter the data requested, and then select **OK**.

To Change Installation Parameters:

1. From the Program Manager window, select the **Lotus Applications** icon.
2. From the Lotus Applications window, select the **1-2-3 Install** icon.
3. When the introductory screen of Install appears, select the **OK** button.
4. From the main menu of Install, select the operation to be performed. (See "Options," below.)

• OPTIONS

Install 1-2-3 Runs the Install program, which transfers files from the distribution disks to your computer system.

View Product Updates Prints late corrections and additions made to the program documentation.

International Options Allows you to change program settings that affect displays of dates, monetary amounts, and other conventions that vary by country.

See Also *Memory Usage*. Part II: *File Printer Setup*.

THE KEYBOARD

Although 1-2-3 for Windows is designed to work best with a mouse, all program selections can be made through the keyboard.

To Control 1-2-3 through the Keyboard:

1. When the Main Menu is displayed at the top of the 1-2-3 application window, press the **Alt** key to activate the menu.
2. Press the key corresponding to the letter underscored in the menu item you want.
3. When the pull-down menu for the item appears, press the key corresponding to the letter underscored in the menu item you want.
   or
   If an accelerator-key equivalent is shown to the right of the menu item you want, press this key or key combination (**Alt** or **Ctrl** plus another key) to bypass the menu system.
4. Repeat step 3 to make a selection from any cascade menu that appears.
5. When a dialog box appears, press **Tab** to move among the options. Use the arrow keys to change the settings. (Pressing Tab repeatedly moves to the right and downward through the options, and Shift-Tab moves to the left and upward.)

6. To activate any labeled button in a dialog box, press **Alt-*letter*,** where the letter key corresponds to the letter underscored in the button label.
7. To complete your work in a dialog box, press ↵ to push the OK button, or **Esc** to push the Cancel button.

To Control an Application Window:

1. When the window is active, press **Alt,** then **spacebar.**
2. Press the letter representing the desired action in the pull-down menu that appears.
3. Press ↵

• NOTES Another way of using the keyboard with 1-2-3 for Windows is to enter 1-2-3 Release 3.1 key commands. Press / or < to activate the Classic menu, then enter the key command sequence.

For specific help on key entry options, select **Help** from the Main Menu, then **Keyboard**.

A table of function keys appears on the inside back cover of this book.

See Also *The Classic Menu, Windows.*

HELP

On-line help is available while you are working with 1-2-3. The Help item on the Main Menu admits you to the same type of menu system used within Windows itself. Pressing **F1** (Help) at any point in the program displays context-sensitive help, or specific information on the current task.

To Get Help:

1. Select **Help** from the Main Menu.

2. Select a command from the Help pull-down menu. (See "Options," below.) Then continue with step 3 under "To Get Help for the Current Task."

To Get Help for the Current Task:

1. Start any task by making the appropriate menu selections. For example, you might select Worksheet, then Delete.
2. Press **F1** (Help). (The Help window appears, in this case containing information on Worksheet Delete.)
3. Select from the Help icons displayed below the Help menu bar to move around the Help system.
4. Continue working on your task, leaving the Help window open for reference. If you wish, move the window by dragging one of its corners.
5. When you are finished using Help, close the Help window by double-clicking on its Control box (top left corner).

• **OPTIONS** Help options appear in three places: on the Help pull-down menu, on a menu bar just below the title bar in the Help window, and in a row of icons just below the menu bar. Select an option from the Help pull-down to view the menu bar and icons.

Help Pull-Down

Index Displays a list of Help topics, or Help index. All parts of the Help system can be accessed through this index.

Using Help Provides information on navigating the Help system.

Keyboard Provides information on key commands used with 1-2-3.

@Functions Brings up information on @function commands, usage, and syntax, including calculations and formulas, within 1-2-3 for Windows. (See "Part IV: @Functions.")

Macros Lists usage, commands, and key names of 1-2-3 macros, or user-defined program routines.

How Do I? Provides information on frequently asked questions about 1-2-3, grouped by task.

For Upgraders Provides cross-references that relate 1-2-3 for Windows selections to Release 3.1 commands.

About 1-2-3... Reports 1-2-3 status information. Displays the version number of the program and a copyright notice, as well as reports on any circular references (such as recursive formulas) in open files. A circular reference refers to itself and can be a source of calculation errors and/or unpredictable results.

Help Menu Bar

File Opens, prints, sets up the printer, or closes Help topics or files.

Edit Pastes (copies) and/or annotates the text of any Help topic to the Clipboard (scratch-pad memory area in Windows).

Bookmark Marks a Help topic so that you can return there easily for future reference.

Help Switches to the Windows Help system.

Help Icon Bar

Index Provides a list of Help topics you can select for information. All parts of the Help system can be accessed through this index.

Back Displays the previous topic you selected. The button is dimmed if you made no previous selections.

Browse (Back or Forward) Two arrow buttons allow you to move backward or forward through the Help system. A button is dimmed if you are at that end of the list.

Search Lets you enter a keyword for a specific topic you want to find. The program will then search through the Help index to find a match for the word you've entered. As an alternative, the Search window includes a list box of available topics. Simply click on any topic in the list box to select it.

MEMORY USAGE

The 1-2-3 for Windows program can use conventional, expanded (LIM), extended, and virtual (RAM disk) memory. The MEM indicator appears on the status line (top right of the screen) when the program may not have enough memory to complete the current operation (<32 Kb). The minimum recommended system RAM for running 1-2-3 for Windows is 2Mb.

To Conserve Memory:

To use less memory in 1-2-3, try one or more of the following steps:

- Avoid large blocks of empty cells in worksheets. Group data-holding cells close to one another.
- Avoid multiple worksheets, or use fewer of them. Combine multiple worksheets, if possible.
- Consolidate memory area.
    1. Save the current worksheet file using **File Save As.**
    2. Reopen the file you just saved with **File Open.**
- Remove unnecessary settings and entries from worksheets with **Range Format Reset.** Use **Worksheet** commands to delete unneeded columns, rows, or sheets. Use **File Extract To** to create a new file containing only the needed data. Save this file and then reopen it, as described above.
- Delete unnecessary formulas. To convert formulas to explicit values, use **Edit Quick Copy Convert to Values.** (Beware of deleting formulas in a chain.)
- Turn off Undo by selecting **Tools User Setup**.
- Close worksheet files you're not working on.
- Avoid formatting or changing settings for ranges larger than 1,000 rows and 100 columns.
- Close all other open windows before trying to save a worksheet file.

- Especially if your hard disk is becoming full, back up and delete unneeded files from your hard disk.
- Avoid use of memory-resident utilities or terminate-and-stay-resident (TSR) programs when using 1-2-3.

• NOTES Both Windows and 1-2-3 use the system driver HIMEM.SYS to manage extended memory. The SMARTDrive utility is used to manage virtual (disk) memory. Normally, the Windows Install program installs these drivers. If the drivers are installed, the following device assignment statements will be found in your system's CONFIG.SYS file (device and path can vary):

device = c:\himem.sys
device = c:\windows\smartdrv.sys *AvgCache MinCache*

AvgCache is the amount of memory, in kilobytes, for the normal cache size. *MinCache* is the minimum cache size.

Some non-Windows applications can use only *expanded* memory and require a different driver. An expanded memory driver that is compatible with Windows and adheres to the LIM standard used with 1-2-3 is EMM386.SYS. If you install this driver, you must observe the following for 1-2-3 to operate properly:

- Don't install this driver unless you have an application (usually a DOS program) that requires it.
- The device assignment command for this driver must appear in the CONFIG.SYS file *after* the assignment statement for HIMEM.SYS. The statement must include a numeric parameter specifying a limit (*MemSize*) on the amount of *extended* memory, in kilobytes, that HIMEM.SYS will allocate to this driver:

  device = c:\windows\emm386.sys *MemSize*

- In Standard or 386 enhanced modes, Windows may be incompatible with some versions of other expanded memory drivers, such as 386-Max, CEMM, or QEMM.

MENUS

Selections in Windows and within the 1-2-3 application appear in a *menu bar* beneath the title bar of a window. A window represents a currently running task or open document. The title bar gives the name of the window.

To Select from a Menu:

1. Click on the menu item you want.
   or
   Drag the pull-down menu from the item in the menu bar, and release when you've highlighted the submenu item you want. Skip step 2.
   or
   Press **Alt**, then the underscored letter of the item you want.
2. Make a command selection from the pull-down menu that appears. Click on the item, or press its underscored letter.
3. If the menu item includes a right arrowhead, a cascade menu containing other selections will appear to the right of the pull-down menu. Make an option selection from the cascade.
4. If a menu item is followed by an ellipsis (...), a dialog box appears. You set options within it by selecting various switches and buttons.

• OPTIONS Selecting a menu item can bring up one of three types of submenus used in Windows. (Any menu item or option that appears with its label *dimmed,* or subdued, is not operable at that point in the program. To activate it, you usually must make some other selection first.)

Pull-Down The submenu of an item on a menu bar. Items listed on the pull-down represent commands, or program selections, and can also correspond to characteristics to be assigned to text or graphics (such as Bold or Italic). A check mark (✓) appearing to the left of an item indicates that it is active. When you click on the item (called a *toggle*) to deactivate it, the check mark disappears.

Cascade If an item in a pull-down menu is followed by an arrowhead, selecting the item will cause a cascading menu to appear just to the right of the pull-down (Figure I.3). A cascading menu is, in effect, a submenu of a submenu. It contains another set of choices.

Dialog Box If an item in a pull-down menu is followed by an ellipsis (...), a dialog box will appear when the item is selected (Figure I.4). A dialog box reports on the current status of program options and prompts you for changes to those options and other inputs.

When a dialog box appears, click on an item to select or reset it. If using the keyboard, press **Tab** to move among the options. (Pressing Tab repeatedly moves to the right and downward through the options, and Shift-Tab moves to the left and upward.) To activate any labeled button, press **Alt-*letter*,** where the letter key corresponds to

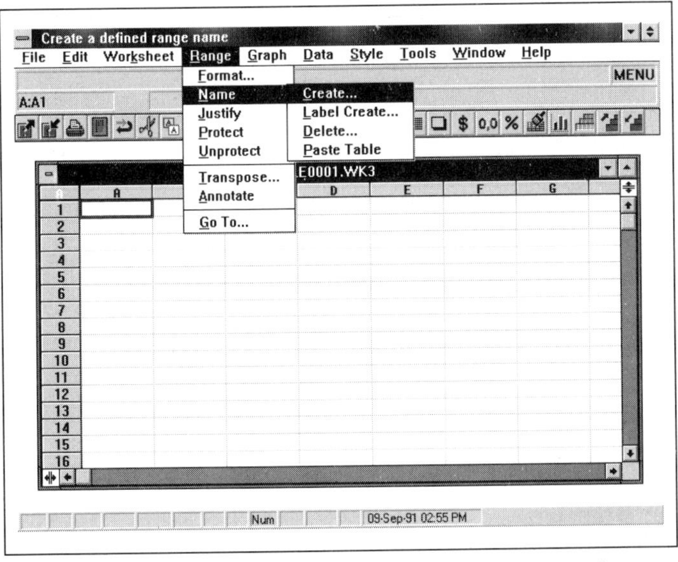

Figure I.3: A cascade menu including the Create command appears when you select Name from the Range pull-down

the letter underscored in the button label. Use the arrow keys to select radio buttons and the spacebar to reset check boxes. In any dialog box, press ↵ to push the OK button, or **Esc** to push the Cancel button.

In Windows, there are six types of controls in a dialog box:

Button A rectangle labeled with an action is a button. Buttons are used primarily as the equivalents of ↵ (Enter) and Esc. A button labeled **OK** or **Continue**... means "Enter," and a button labeled **Cancel** means "Esc." Other buttons might appear for actions such as Save, Retrieve, and so on.

Toggle A selection that can be only On/Off or Yes/No is indicated by a hollow square. If the square contains an X, the toggle is On; if the square is empty, the toggle is Off. A toggle can be set individually, separate from other options. In 1-2-3, toggles are sometimes called *check boxes*. A check box that is solid, or filled in, is not available or not applicable with current settings.

Radio button A small, hollow circle next to an option name is a radio button, which can also be On or Off. If On, the circle contains a black dot. Radio buttons appear in sets and, like the controls on an old car's push-button radio, only one option in the set can be On at any given time.

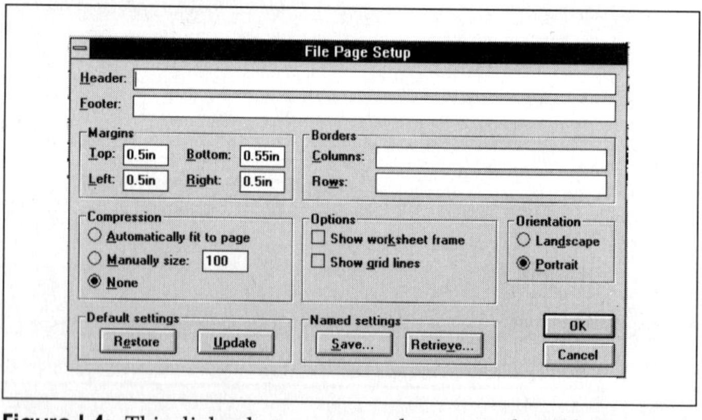

Figure I.4: This dialog box appears when you select File Page Setup

List box A box that contains a list of options or names, such as devices or file names. Entries inside the box can scroll so that lists can extend beyond the borders of the box. You select an item in the list by clicking on it. You can scroll the list by clicking on or dragging the sliders or arrows on the side of the box.

Drop-down box A list box may be condensed to a single line that expands, or drops down, to show a longer list when you click on it.

Text box Fields in which you can enter data are text boxes. Click on the box to make it active; a blinking vertical-bar cursor appears. Key in the data. The dialog box usually contains a button for continuing, which has the same effect as pressing ↵ to accept the entry.

MINIMIZE/MAXIMIZE

In Windows and 1-2-3, application (task) or document (worksheet) windows can be minimized (shrunk to an icon) or maximized (enlarged to fill the desktop). Minimize a window to keep it ready while making room on the desktop for other windows and/or to reduce its processing priority or memory allocation. Maximize a window to have more room to work within it and/or to give it higher processing priority and more memory.

To Minimize or Maximize a Window:

1. Click on either the **Minimize (▼)** or **Maximize (▲)** buttons in the top right corner of the window's title bar (Figure I.5). Omit step 2.

   or

   Press **Alt-hyphen** to activate the window's Control menu.

2. From the Control pull-down menu, select **Minimize** or **Maximize.**

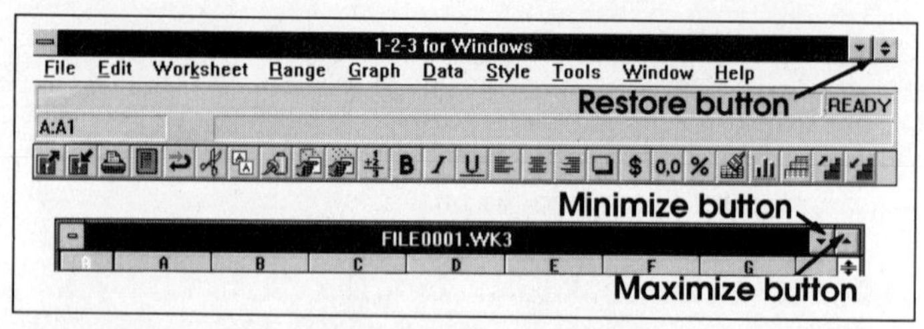

Figure I.5: Minimize (▼) and Maximize (▲) buttons are found in the top right corner of any window

To Restore a Window to Its Previous Size:

1. If the window has been shrunk to an icon, double-click on the icon. If the window has been maximized, double-click on the **Restore** button in the top right corner of its menu bar. Omit step 2.

   or

   Press **Alt-hyphen** to activate the window's Control-menu box.

2. From the Control pull-down menu, select **Restore.**

• **NOTE** In step 1, if the window is the 1-2-3 application window itself or any dialog box, the keyboard command for accessing its Control menu is **Alt-spacebar.**

THE MOUSE

Like the Windows environment, the 1-2-3 for Windows program is designed for convenient input with a single-button mouse, or pointing device. (Optionally, a two-button mouse can be used for drawing actions.) Mouse actions include clicking (point and press the button once), double-clicking (point and click twice rapidly), and dragging (point, press and hold, move to new location, and release).

To Make Selections with a Mouse:

1. Click on the menu name in the control bar.
2. The pull-down menu for that item appears. Move the pointer to the submenu item desired and click on it.

or

1. Move the pointer to the menu name in the control bar.
2. Press and hold down the mouse button as the pull-down menu appears. Still holding the button down, move the pointer to the submenu item desired, then release the button. That is, make the selection in a single action by *dragging* the pull-down menu and releasing on the desired item.

To Change Dialog Box Settings:

1. When a dialog box appears, click on any button, toggle, or radio button to reset or activate it.
2. Click on any list box or drop-down box to activate it. Drag a list to scroll it and release to select the highlighted item.
   or
   Double-click on any list item to select it.
3. Click on a text box to activate it. A flashing vertical bar appears at the insertion point. Key in the text data required.
4. When you have finished making entries in a dialog box, click on the **OK** or **Continue**... button. To reset the options and return to the previous menu, click on the **Cancel** button.

To Specify Cells and Ranges:

- Click on a cell to select it. The cell will be highlighted and its address and contents will appear in the boxes in the top left corner of the screen.

or

- To select a range, click on a cell in one corner of the range and drag the pointer to the opposite corner. The range will be highlighted.

To Scroll the Display:

- Drag the slider (square button) in the scroll box until the display is adjusted to suit you.

or

- To scroll the display one line or increment at a time, click on either of the arrow buttons at the ends of the scroll box. Repeat until the display is adjusted to suit you.

See Also *The Control Menu, Menus, Minimize/Maximize, Windows.*

WINDOWS

Any application (task) window or document (worksheet) window within 1-2-3 can be moved or adjusted in size on the desktop, or screen.

To Move a Window:

1. Drag the title bar of the window to the new position. Omit steps 2–4.

   or

   Press **Alt-hyphen** to activate the window's Control menu.
2. From the Control pull-down, select **Move.**
3. Use the arrow keys (←↑↓→) to move the window to the new position.
4. Press ↵.

To Resize a Window:

1. Drag one of the borders or corners of the window to a new position.
   or
   Press **Alt-hyphen** to activate the window's Control menu.
2. From the Control pull-down, select **Size.**
3. Use the arrow keys (←↑↓→) to move the window's borders to new positions.
4. Press ↵.

• NOTES The 1-2-3 application window itself cannot be moved or resized. To gain control of a dialog box when using the keyboard in step 1, press **Alt-spacebar** instead.

See Also *The Control Menu, Minimize/Maximize.*

Part Two

The Main Menu

This portion covers the core capabilities of Lotus 1-2-3 for Windows. Most commands appear as items in pull-down submenus from the Main Menu bar, also called the *Worksheet menu*. Proceeding from left to right across the menu bar, the pull-downs are: File, Edit, Worksheet, Range, Graph, Data, Style, Tools, Window, and Help.

The Help menu in 1-2-3 is an extension of the Windows Help system. Navigating this system is covered in Part I of this book.

The Graph menu is so extensive that it has its own menu bar. The Graph pull-down entries from the Main Menu, as well as the Graph Window menu itself, are covered separately in Part III.

ACCELERATOR KEYS

Certain key combinations can be used to execute 1-2-3 commands in a single operation from the keyboard, bypassing the menu system. For example, pressing Ctrl-Ins executes the command Edit Copy. These accelerator keys are listed on the inside back cover of this book. Accelerator-key equivalents also appear opposite the command items in pull-down menus.

DATA CONNECT TO EXTERNAL (DATALENS)

Establishes a connection with a table in an external database system so that you can execute subsequent Data Query and Data External Options commands. (The program feature that permits you to query external databases such as dBASE IV, Paradox, and SQL is called *DataLens*.)

To Connect to an External Database:

1. From the Main Menu bar, select **Data.**
2. From the Data pull-down, select **Connect to External.**
3. In the Data Connect to External dialog box, select the database driver name from the Connect to Driver list box.
   or
   Key in the database driver, database, and table (separated by spaces) in the Connect to Driver text box, and skip steps 4 and 5.
4. Select the database name from the Connect to Database list box.
5. Select the table from the Connect to Table list box.

6. Enter a range name that will be assigned to the table during your 1-2-3 session.
7. To connect to an additional database, first select **Connect**, then repeat steps 4–6. To connect to another table in the same database, repeat only steps 5 and 6.
8. Select **OK.**

To Disconnect from an External Database/Table:

1. From the Main Menu bar, select **Data.**
2. From the Data pull-down, select **External Options.**
3. From the External Options cascade, select **Disconnect.**
4. In the Data External Options dialog box, select the table name to be disconnected, then select **OK.**
5. To exit the database, select the database to be disconnected, then select **OK.**

• **NOTES** When you select Connect, if prompted by the program, enter a user ID and password for the system you have selected. If the prompt appears but identification is not required, simply select **OK** or press ↵.

In step 3 of Connect to External, if the driver was not added to your system by Install 1-2-3, the program will prompt you to insert a diskette that holds the required driver file.

Users of dBASE IV should make a copy of the source file before connecting to it through 1-2-3 to avoid making unwanted changes to the file.

Users of SQL must first create an external table using Data External Options Create Table.

See Also *Data External Options, Data Query*. Part I: *Install 1-2-3*.

DATA DISTRIBUTION

Generates a frequency distribution of the values in a selected range. A frequency distribution is a count of the number of data values in the range that fall within specified limits, or bounds. The range to be counted is the *value range* and the limits are the *bin range.* The purpose is to highlight patterns in the data.

To Generate a Frequency Distribution:

1. Select two blank columns in the current worksheet. The left column will hold the bin range.
2. Enter the limit intervals in the bin range in ascending order.
3. Highlight a value range to be counted.
4. From the Main Menu bar, select **Data.**
5. From the Data pull-down, select **Distribution.**
6. If you wish to override the value range selected in step 3, specify a range name or address in the Values text box.
7. In the Bin text box, enter the bin range.
8. Select **OK.**

• **NOTES** The program places the distribution counts in the blank column to the right of the bin range. The number at the bottom of this column is a count of values greater than the bin maximum.

Enter only numeric values as bin intervals in step 2 and omit blanks.

DATA EXTERNAL OPTIONS CREATE TABLE

In some cases, the database driver you select with Data Connect to External (DataLens) can create a table to hold the data that you extract. However, with some systems, including SQL, you must use this command first to create the table before connecting to the database. The command sets up a table definition that contains information on field names and widths, and data types. Optionally, you can use an existing table in 1-2-3 as a model, or you can modify the definition of an existing external table.

To Define a Table Using a Model in 1-2-3:

1. Open the 1-2-3 file that contains the database table to be used as a model. (See "Notes," below.)
   or
   Build a new database table in the current worksheet.
2. From the Main Menu bar, select **Data.**
3. From the Data pull-down, select **External Options.**
4. From the External Options cascade, select **Create Table.**
5. In the Data External Options Create Table dialog box, connect to the database driver and database. (Steps are the same as in "Data Connect to External (DataLens).")
6. When prompted by the program, enter a name for the new table in the external database and a range name to be used for it in 1-2-3.
7. In the Model Range text box, enter the worksheet range of the 1-2-3 database table.
8. In the Output Range text box, enter a worksheet range to hold the table definition. (The address of the first cell is sufficient.)

9. If your database driver requires a setup string to create the table, enter the string in the Table Creation String text box. (See "Options," below.)
10. Select **OK**.

• NOTES To modify an existing table definition rather than using a model in 1-2-3, see "Data External Options Paste Fields."

In 1-2-3, a *database table* is a range that contains one column for each field of a typical database record, ordered from left to right in the order the fields appear in the database records. The top row in the table contains column-heading labels that are used as field names. Column widths correspond to field lengths, and cell formatting controls data typing.

The model is translated into a table definition. The table definition that is passed to the DataLens driver must have six columns, from left to right: Field names, Data types, Field widths, Field labels, Field descriptions, and Field creation strings (see "Options," below). SQL and dBASE IV drivers use only columns 1–3 and 6. Paradox uses only columns 1–3. In any case, however, columns 4 and 5 must be present.

• OPTIONS Paradox users must supply one of the following setup strings in step 8 to determine the sort order for the table: SORT ASCII, SORT INTL (international ASCII), SORT NORDAN (Norwegian and Danish), or SORT SWEDFIN (Swedish and Finnish).

See Also *Data Connect to External (DataLens), Data External Options Paste Fields.*

DATA EXTERNAL OPTIONS PASTE FIELDS

Permits you to modify an existing database table definition prior to connecting to an external database through Data Connect to

External (DataLens). In some cases, the database driver creates the table automatically, making this command unnecessary.

To Modify a Table for DataLens:

1. Open a worksheet document window to contain the new table.
2. From the Main Menu bar, select **Data.**
3. From the Data pull-down, select **External Options.**
4. From the External Options cascade, select **Paste Table.**
5. The Data External Options Paste Fields dialog box appears and a list of connected database tables is displayed in the list box. Select the table name to be modified. The name is displayed in the Connected Tables text box.
6. In the Range text box, enter a range in the current worksheet to hold a copy of the table.
7. Select **OK.**
8. A copy of the table appears in the current worksheet. Edit the table in 1-2-3.
9. Enter **/Data External Create Name** from the 1-2-3 Classic menu.
10. Select the name of the database driver and database name to be used with the table.
11. Key in a name for the new table.
12. If required by the driver you are using, enter a setup string for the table.
13. Select **Definition Use-Definition** and enter the range of the new table definition.
14. Select **Go.**

• **NOTES** The database table definition that is passed to the DataLens driver must have six columns, from left to right: Field names, Data types, Field widths, Field labels, Field descriptions, and

Field creation strings (see "Options," below). SQL and dBASE IV drivers use only columns 1–3 and 6. Paradox uses only columns 1–3. In any case, however, columns 4 and 5 must be present.

Modify the parameters in the table definition to match the external database records in your application. You might also wish to modify a table definition to specify some fields as index fields for use with Paradox.

See Also *Data Connect to External (DataLens), Data External Options Create Table.*

DATA EXTERNAL OPTIONS SEND COMMAND

Permits you to send command strings to an external database system through the DataLens driver connecting it to 1-2-3.

To Send Commands to an External Database System:

1. Connect to the external database system. (See "Data Connect to External (DataLens).")
2. From the Main Menu bar, select **Data.**
3. From the Data pull-down, select **External Options.**
4. From the External Options cascade, select **Send Command.**
5. In the Data External Options Send Command dialog box, enter the command in the Command String text box.
6. Select **OK.**

• NOTES If you omit step 1, follow the steps that appear in the dialog box in step 5 for connecting to the external database. Specify the DataLens driver, database name, and table as described in the entry "Data Connect to External (DataLens)."

If you are connected to dBASE IV or SQL, the command string entered in step 5 can be any command valid in the database system. You cannot issue commands to Paradox from within 1-2-3.

See Also *Data Connect to External (DataLens), Data Query.*

DATA FILL

Fills a specified range with data values generated from the starting (Start) to ending (Stop) values you enter, each value increasing according to an increment (Step).

To Fill a Range with Incremented Data:

1. In the current worksheet window, highlight a range to hold the data.
2. From the Main Menu bar, select **Data.**
3. From the Data pull-down, select **Fill.**
4. The Data Fill dialog box appears. If you wish to override the range selected in step 1, specify a range name or address in the Range text box.
5. Enter values for Start (starting value), Step (increment), and Stop (ending value).
6. Select **OK.**

• NOTES This command overwrites any data in the selected range.

In step 5, valid entries include numeric values, percentages, dates, or times. Start and Stop values must be of the same data type, and the Step must be a valid way of counting that type. Optionally, you can enter formulas, range names, or cell addresses that result in or contain values. To generate a set of values that decreases from Start to Stop, enter a negative Step value and make sure that Start is greater than Step. Precede the range name with + or – in the text box in step 5.

Ranges are filled in top-to-bottom, left-to-right, sheet-by-sheet order.

Dates in Short International format are not valid with this command.

For dates, you can use the following letter suffixes as Step values: d (day), w (week), m (month), q (quarter), or y (year). For time, use s (seconds), min (minutes), or h (hours).

DATA MATRIX INVERT

Generates the mathematical inverse of values in a matrix. For example, the inverse of *N/M* would be *M/N*. The matrix must be a square range (same number of columns and rows).

To Invert a Matrix:

1. In the current worksheet window, highlight the range that holds the matrix.
2. From the Main Menu bar, select **Data.**
3. From the Data pull-down, select **Matrix.**
4. From the Matrix cascade, select **Invert.**
5. The Data Matrix Invert dialog box appears. If you wish to override the range selected in step 1, specify a range name or address in the From text box.
6. In the To text box, enter a range to hold the inverted matrix. (The address of the first cell is sufficient.)
7. Select **OK.**

• NOTES This command overwrites the range you specify in step 6.

Take care that matrices, which must be square for use with this command, contain no more than 80 cells on a side. Avoid including values of greatly different magnitudes.

The matrix you specify in step 5 need not be in a file that is currently open. Precede the range name with a valid device, path, and file name enclosed in double angle brackets (<< >>).

You can invert three-dimensional ranges. Matrices are inverted sheet by sheet; results are placed in the same sheet.

A primary purpose of using matrix arithmetic is to solve simultaneous algebraic equations. In matrix analysis, inversion often is used as the first step in performing matrix multiplication. (See "Data Matrix Multiply.")

See Also *Data Matrix Multiply.*

DATA MATRIX MULTIPLY

Multiplies one matrix by another, placing the results in a new, third matrix. A matrix is a square range (same number of columns and rows). The matrices selected must be the same size.

To Perform Matrix Multiplication:

1. From the Main Menu bar, select **Data.**
2. From the Data pull-down, select **Matrix.**
3. From the Matrix cascade, select **Multiply.**
4. The Data Matrix Multiply dialog box appears. In the First Matrix text box, enter the range that holds the first matrix.
5. In the Second Matrix text box, enter the range that holds the second matrix (the multiplier).

6. In the Output Matrix text box, enter a range to hold the results. (The address of the first cell is sufficient.)
7. Select **OK.**

• NOTES This command overwrites the range in step 6.

Matrices need not be square to be multiplied, but the number of columns in the first matrix must equal the number of rows in the second, and the product of these cannot exceed 6,553 cells. Neither matrix can have more than 80 cells on a side (columns or rows). The output range will have the same number of rows as the first matrix and the same number of columns as the second.

The matrices you specify in steps 4 and 5 need not be in files that are currently open. Precede the range name with a valid device, path, and file name enclosed in double angle brackets (<< >>).

See Also *Data Matrix Invert.*

DATA PARSE

Used after File Import From Text to convert long labels into multiple columns of data in the current worksheet.

To Parse Long Labels:

1. Import text data from an external file into the current worksheet with **File Import From Text.**
2. Move the cell pointer to a cell that contains a long label.
3. From the Main Menu bar, select **Data.**
4. From the Data pull-down, select **Parse.**
5. The Data Parse dialog box appears. Select the **Create** button.
6. A new row containing a format line is inserted in the worksheet above the long label. Edit the format line so

that each column matches the width and data type of a corresponding string in the long label.

7. In the Data Parse dialog box, enter the address of the first cell in the first column containing a new format line.
8. In the Output Range text box, enter a range to hold the parsed data.
9. Select **OK.**

• NOTES The parsed data generated by this command overwrite the specified output range.

To clear the range entries so that you can enter new information, select the **Reset** button in the dialog box before you select **OK.**

If the imported text lines vary in format, select **Cancel** after step 6, repeat steps 3–6, and create another format line for the next long label.

See Also *Range Format, Worksheet Column Width.*

DATA QUERY

Permits you to perform various operations on database tables. In 1-2-3, a *database table* is a range that contains one column for each field of a typical database record, ordered from left to right in the order the fields appear in the database records. The top row in the table contains column-heading labels that are used as field names. Column widths correspond to field lengths, and cell formatting controls data typing.

To Query Database Tables:

1. From the Main Menu bar, select **Data.**
2. From the Data pull-down, select **Query.**

3. The Data Query dialog box appears. In the Input Range text box, specify range(s) that hold 1-2-3 database tables.
4. In the Criteria Range text box, enter a range that holds criteria for record selection from the database table.
5. In the Output Range text box, specify a range that will hold the selected records.
6. If you wish to extract records from the database, select the **Extract Unique Only** check box to specify that there will be no duplications.
7. Also in the dialog box, select the type of query to be performed: **Find, Delete, Extract**, or **Modify.**
8. If you selected Modify in step 6, the Data Query Modify Dialog box appears. Select **Extract, Replace, Insert**, or **Finish.**

• **NOTES** You can query an external table as the input range to this command if you have first connected to the database system through Data Connect External. To do this, it may be necessary first to build a table definition with Data External Options Create Table or Data External Options Paste Fields.

To access multiple database tables, enter table names separated by commas in the Input Range text box in step 3.

The criteria range in step 4 contains at least two rows. In the first row, enter one field name for each column, just as the field names appear in the database table. In the second and any subsequent rows, enter selection criteria under each field name, including logical operators (such as =, >, or <) and labels, values, or formulas. If you omit criteria for any field name in the criteria range, the program selects all records.

Enter field names in the first row of the output range you specify in step 5. You can also enter formulas in the output range if you wish the results to be calculated.

• OPTIONS Buttons in the dialog box in step 6 include the following:

Find Searches the database table and locates records that match the specified criteria. When a record is located, the FIND mode indicator appears and the program highlights the record in the table. Press ↓ or ↑ to move among records in the table, and ← and → to move among fields within records. Press **Home** and **End** to move to the first and last records, respectively. In FIND mode, press **F2** (Edit) to edit the record. Press **F7** (Query) once to return to READY mode, and again to repeat Data Query Find. Press **Esc** or ↵ to return to the Data Query dialog box.

Delete Causes any record matching the search criteria to be deleted from the database table. Also deletes any blank rows.

Extract Copies selected records from the database table to the output range you specify. The program will join fields that are held in common by two or more database tables. To do this, include a *join formula* in the corresponding field column in the criteria range. (The syntax of a join formula is *+table1.field1=table2.field2.*) To transform the data that are extracted, enter formulas into the corresponding locations in the output range. Any formulas in the input range are converted to values. To assure no duplicates in extracted records, perform step 6 above.

Modify Copies the selected records and permits you to edit them before they are written to the output range. Its options, in step 8, are the following:

> **Extract** Removes the records from the database table but does not delete their positions. You can then reinsert them with the Replace button.
>
> **Replace** Reinserts edited records retrieved with Modify Extract in the database table (insert range). Edit records when they are in the output range.
>
> **Insert** Places new records added to the output range in the database table (insert range).
>
> **Finish** Ends Data Query Modify.

Reset Clears the entries in the Insert, Criteria, and Output Range text boxes so that you can enter new information for another query operation.

See Also *Data Connect to External (DataLens), Data External Options Create Table, Data External Options Paste Fields.*

DATA REGRESSION

Performs multiple linear regression analysis. In performing data regression, the program compares two sets of data, or ranges. The first set, or *X range,* is the independent variable, and the second set, or *Y range,* is the dependent variable. Statistics from the comparison are placed in the output range you specify. A best-fit straight line of X-Y points is calculated to determine the slope, or trend, of the data.

To Perform Data Regression Analysis:

1. From the Main Menu bar, select **Data.**
2. From the Data pull-down, select **Regression.**
3. The Data Regression dialog box appears. In the X-Range text box, enter the range containing the X values, or independent variable.
4. In the Y-Range text box, enter the range containing the Y values, or dependent variable.
5. In the Output Range text box, enter a range to hold the calculated results. (The address of the first cell is sufficient.)
6. Select one of the radio buttons, **Compute** or **Set to Zero,** for the Y-intercept calculation.
7. To enter new ranges in steps 3–5, select **Reset** and repeat those steps.
8. Select **OK.**

• NOTES The results generated by this command overwrite the cells in the output range.

The maximum number of columns in the X range is 75. These must be adjacent to one another. The Y range must be one column with the same number of rows as the X range.

Results placed in the output range include:

Y-axis intercept (a numeric value)

degrees of freedom (number of observations – number of X values – 1)

number of observations (number of rows in X and Y ranges)

R^2 value (reliability of the analysis)

standard error of the X coefficients

standard error of the Y estimate

X coefficients (slope for each X variable)

• OPTIONS In step 6, selecting Compute calculates the point at which the regression line (trend) intersects the Y axis. If you select Set to Zero, the Y-axis intercept is assumed to be zero. (This is true only if zero values in the X range would result in zeros in the Y range. If you set this incorrectly, the R^2 value reported will be negative.)

See Also *Part III: The Graph Window Menu.*

DATA SORT

Rearranges data in a range in the order you specify, such as alphabetic or numeric, ascending or descending.

To Sort Data in a Range:

1. In the current worksheet window, highlight a range (data table) of records to be sorted.
2. From the Main Menu bar, select **Data.**

3. From the Data pull-down, select **Sort.**
4. If you wish to override the range selected in step 1, specify a range name or address in the Data Range text box.
5. In the Primary Key text box, enter the top cell address of the first column in the database table containing the field name by which records will be sorted.
6. For the primary key, select **Ascending** or **Descending** for the order of the resulting list.
7. Optionally, to specify a subordinate order, enter a column address and sort order for a secondary key.
8. Optionally, to specify further levels for sorting, select the **Extra Keys** button and enter the key, key range, and sort order in the Data Sort Extra Keys dialog box. Select **Add Key** for each level added, then select **OK.**
9. To enter new ranges in steps 4, 5, 7, and 8, select **Reset** and repeat steps 4–8.
10. In the Data Sort dialog box, select **OK.**

• NOTES If the range you specify in step 1 is a database table, omit the first row containing the field names from the range address.

An example of a *primary key* would be a person's last name; the secondary key could be the first name. Extra keys might correspond to middle initials, ZIP codes, and so on.

• OPTIONS You can add multiple levels of keys in the Data Sort Extra Keys dialog box in step 8. For each level, specify the number of the level in the Key text box and the database-table column of the sort key in the Key Range text box. Select **Ascending** or **Descending** order. Select **Add Key** to add the key to the list, and repeat the process until all numbered, subordinate sort keys have been defined. Then select **OK.**

DATA WHAT-IF TABLE

Substitutes values for 1–3 variables in a formula (called *1-, 2-,* or *3-way analysis*). Two types of calculations can be performed: sensitivity analysis or cross-tabulation. In sensitivity analysis, variables in formulas are simply substituted and the results output to a range. In cross-tabulation, a database @function is applied to a database table. The purpose of what-if analysis is to test the results of different assumptions on a formula or set of formulas.

To Perform Sensitivity Analysis:

1. Identify a table range in the current worksheet to hold the table that will be generated. (If you specify 3-way analysis, compose the table of multiple, contiguous sheets.)
2. Select a location outside this range for 1–3 input cells. Label the cells so that you can refer to them in later steps. Leave the contents of the cell(s) blank. (One cell is required for each dimension of the analysis: 1 cell for 1-way, 2 cells for 2-way, 3 cells for 3-way.)
3. In the worksheet, enter the formula(s) to be analyzed. (See "Notes," below, for specific locations for each type of analysis.)
4. Enter values into the table range. (See "Notes," below, for requirements.)
5. From the Main Menu bar, select **Data.**
6. From the Data pull-down, select **What-if Table.**
7. From the What-if Table cascade, select **1-**, **2-**, or **3-Way.** (See "Notes," below.)
8. In the Data What-If Table dialog box, enter the range you set up in step 1 in the Table Range text box.
9. For 3-way analysis only, enter the cell address that holds the formula to analyze in the Formula Cell text box.

10. Enter the cell addresses of the input cells in text boxes Input Cell 1–3.
11. Select **OK.**

To Perform Cross-Tabulation:

1. Identify a database table (special type of 1-2-3 range) that holds the records to be analyzed. (See "Notes," below.)
2. Set up a table range in the current worksheet. For 3-way analysis, you will need multiple sheets, one for each value to be input to the third variable.
3. Set up a criteria range. (See "Notes.")
4. Select a cell outside the table range and enter a database @function to be applied to the table.
5. Perform steps 4–11 above.

To Reset Ranges:

1. Move the cell pointer into the file document window that contains the what-if tables to be reset.
2. From the Main Menu bar, select **Data.**
3. From the Data pull-down, select **What-if Table.**
4. From the What-if Table cascade, select **Reset.**
5. All input cell, formula, and table ranges in the what-if tables in the file will be cleared.

• **NOTES** In 1-2-3, a *database table* is a range that contains one column for each field of a typical database record. The requirements for setting up table ranges for sensitivity analysis and cross-tabulation differ. Requirements also vary by the number of dimensions involved in the analysis.

Sensitivity Analysis Input-cell addresses or their labels should be used as variable names in your formulas. You never enter data directly into the input cells. The program uses them as buffers, and each input cell must be referenced in each formula to be tested.

You enter data values in the table range; the program places the results of the analysis there, as well. The table range must be set up in steps 3 and 4 as follows:

1-way analysis Leave the cell in the top left corner of the table range blank. Enter the formula(s) to be analyzed in the remaining cells in the first row. Enter the data values that will be substituted in the formula in the first column, starting at the second cell (top left cell blank). (See Figure II.1.)

2-way analysis Enter a single formula in the top left cell of the table range. The formula must refer to both of the input cells you set up in step 2. In the first column (starting with the second cell, beneath the formula), enter the data values to be substituted for input cell 1. In the row to the right of the formula, enter the data values to be substituted for input cell 2. Results for each pair of variables will be displayed at the intersection of the corresponding column and row in the table range. (See Figure II.2.)

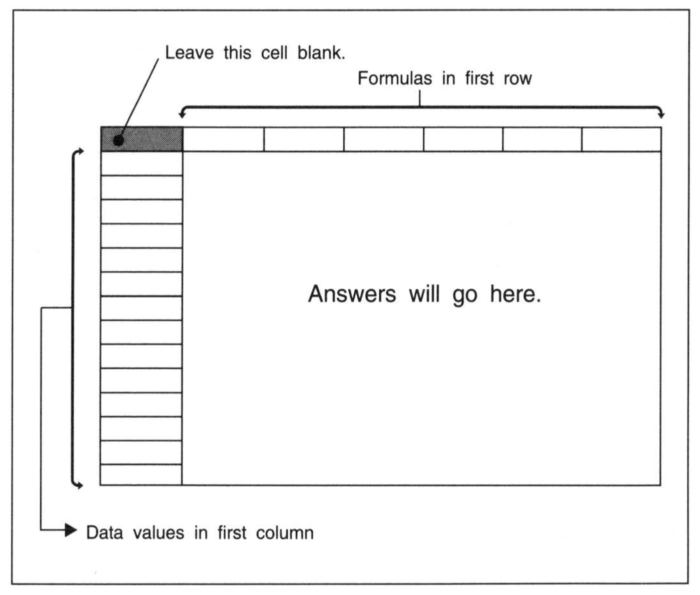

Figure II.1: 1-way sensitivity analysis

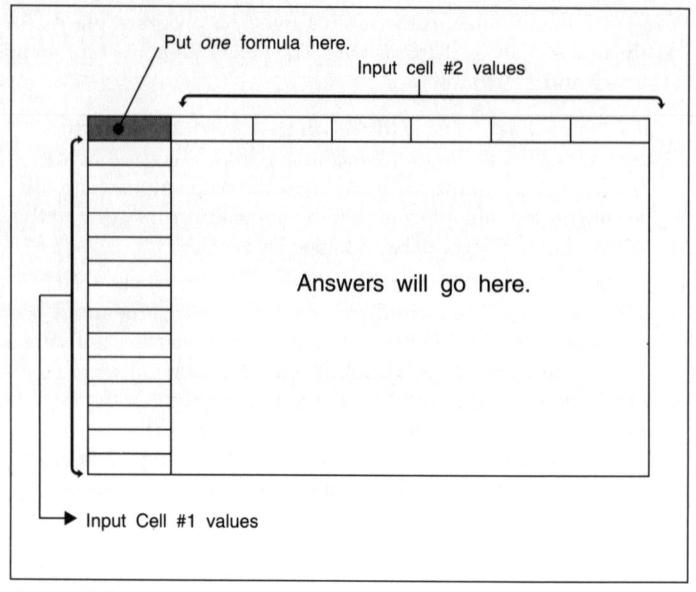

Figure II.2: 2-way sensitivity analysis

3-way analysis Compose the table range of multiple sheets (three-dimensional range). You will need a sheet for each data value you enter for the third input cell, or variable. Enter a single formula at a location *outside* of the table range. The formula must refer to each of the three input cells you set up in step 2. When you begin to build the table range, leave the top left cell in all sheets blank. In the first column of the first sheet (starting with the second cell), enter data values for input cell 1. Use **Edit Quick Copy** to copy this column of data to all the other sheets in the table range. In the first row of the first sheet, enter data values for input cell 2. Copy this row to all sheets. Finally, enter the data values for input cell 3 in the top left cell of each sheet. Results are shown in the cell at the three-dimensional intersection of the three variables. (See Figure II.3.)

Cross-Tabulation In cross-tabulation, each database @function must use the database table as its input range, a field name ("*fieldname*") for data values, and the criteria range. (The input range can be an external table.) You specify labels or values from the

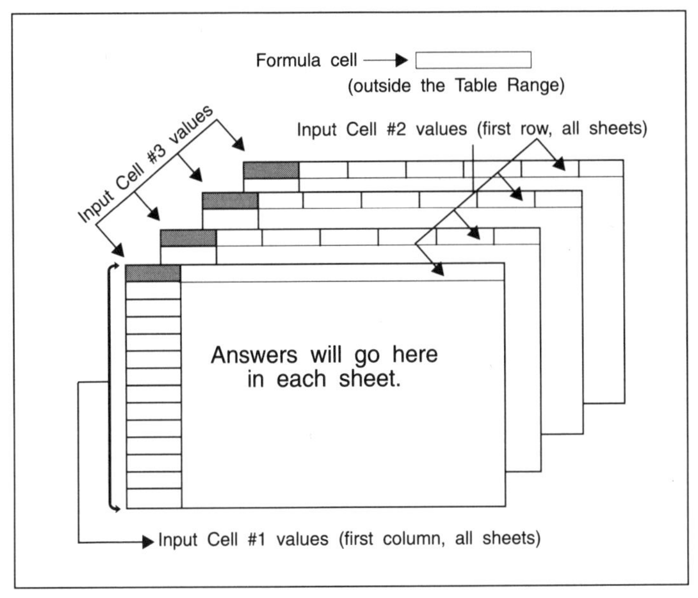

Figure II.3: 3-way sensitivity analysis

database as data values in the table range. (You never make entries directly into the input cells. The program uses them as buffers.) Results are displayed in the table range. To begin building the criteria range and table range, in step 3, create a two-row criteria range that does not lie within the table range. Further steps are as follows:

1-way analysis Copy one field name (the selection criterion) from the database table to one of the blank rows. The cell just below it will be the input cell (enter this address in step 10). In the table range, leave the cell in the top left corner blank. Enter one or more database @functions in the remaining cells in the first row. Enter the data values to be used in the tabulation in the first column, starting at the second cell (top left cell blank). (See Figure II.4.)

2-way analysis Copy two field names (the selection criteria) from the database table to one of the blank rows. The cells just

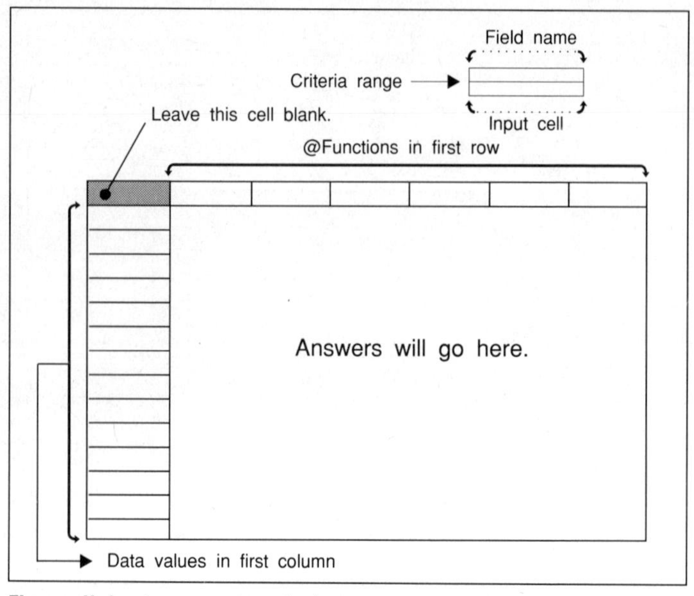

Figure II.4: 1-way cross-tabulation

below each field name are input cells 1 and 2 (enter these addresses in step 10). In the table range, enter a single database @function in the top left cell. In the first column (starting with the second cell, beneath the formula) enter the data values for input cell 1. In the row to the right of the formula, enter the data values for input cell 2. Results for each pair of variables will be displayed at the intersection of the corresponding column and row in the table range. (See Figure II.5)

3-way analysis Copy three field names (the selection criteria) from the database table to one of the blank rows. The cells just below each field name are input cells 1, 2, and 3 (enter these addresses in step 10). Compose the table range of multiple sheets (three-dimensional range). You will need a sheet for each data value you enter for the third input cell, or variable. Enter a single database @function at a location *outside* the

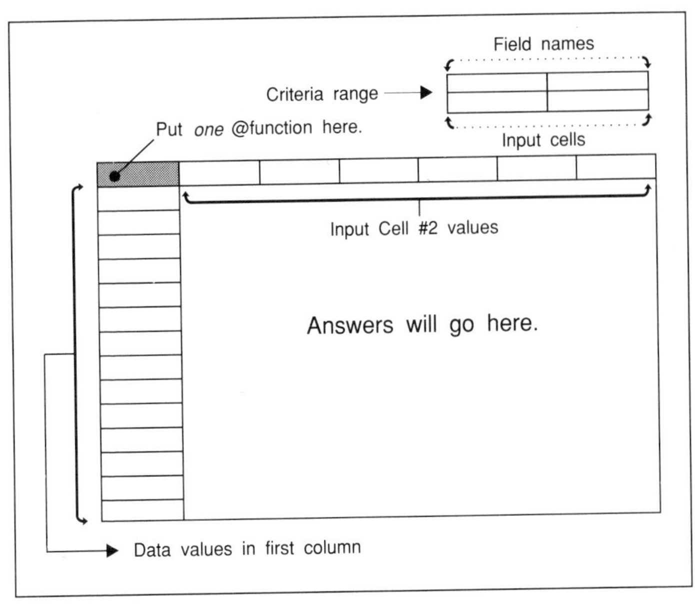

Figure II.5: 2-way cross-tabulation

criteria and table ranges. When you begin to build the table range, leave the top left cell in all sheets blank. In the first column of the first sheet (starting with the second cell), enter data values for input cell 1. Use **Edit Quick Copy** to copy this column of data to all the other sheets in the table range. In the first row of the first sheet, enter data values for input cell 2. Copy this row to all sheets. Finally, enter the data values for input cell 3 in the top left cell of each sheet. Results are shown in the cell at the three-dimensional intersection of the three variables. (See Figure II.6.)

Consider using Data Query Extract instead of this cross-tabulation function when working with large databases.

See Also *Data Connect to External (DataLens), Data Query.*

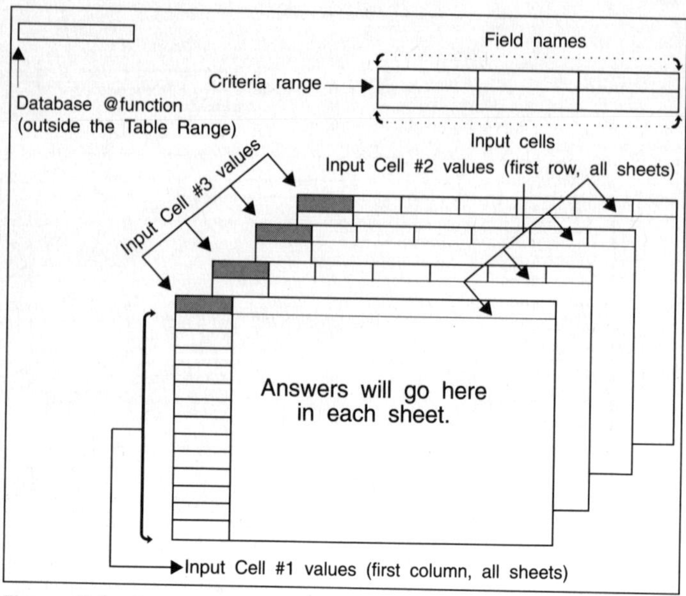

Figure II.6: 3-way cross-tabulation

EDIT CLEAR

Deletes the contents of the highlighted cell or range in the current worksheet. Cleared data include numeric values, text, graphs, formulas, and formatting. The affected cells remain in the worksheet and contain blanks.

To Delete Data from a Worksheet:

1. Highlight the cell or range from which data will be cleared.
2. From the Main Menu bar, select **Edit.**

   or

   Press **Del** and skip step 3.
3. From the Edit pull-down, select **Clear.**

• **NOTES** To undo a deletion, select **Edit Undo** or press **Alt-Backspace** before you make another deletion.

Using Edit Clear does not affect the contents of the Clipboard or any cells that have been protected.

A graph will not be deleted if any part of it lies outside the range you select in step 1.

To clear data and also move it to the Clipboard, use **Edit Cut** instead. To clear types of data selectively from the worksheet, use **Edit Clear Special.**

See Also *Edit Clear Special, Edit Cut, Edit Undo.* Part I: *The Clipboard.*

EDIT CLEAR SPECIAL

Clears, or deletes, selected types of data from a highlighted cell or range in the current worksheet.

To Delete Selected Data Types:

1. Highlight the cell or range from which data will be cleared.
2. From the Main Menu bar, select **Edit.**
3. From the Edit pull-down, select **Clear Special.**
4. In the Edit Clear Special dialog box, select the types of data to be cleared. (See "Options," below.)
5. The range you selected in step 1 should appear in the Range field of the dialog box. If you wish, you can select a different range by entering a new range name or address here in the text box.
6. Select **OK.**

• **NOTES** This command does not affect the contents of the Clipboard or any cells that have been protected.

To undo this command, use **Edit Undo** before you perform another deletion. To delete all data in a cell or range, use **Edit Clear** instead. To delete all data and move them to the Clipboard in one command, use **Edit Cut.**

• **OPTIONS** In step 4, select any or all of the check boxes to indicate the type of data to be cleared: **Cell Contents** (retains format), **Number Format** (resets to defaults), **Style** (resets to defaults), or **Graph** (retains the data). For a graph to be deleted, it must lie entirely within the range you specified in step 1.

See Also *Edit Clear, Edit Cut*. Part I: *The Clipboard.*

EDIT COPY

Copies the contents of a highlighted cell or range in the current worksheet to the Clipboard, a scratch-pad memory area in Windows that can be used to pass data among different documents and programs.

To Copy to the Clipboard:

1. Highlight the cell or range from which data will be copied.
2. From the Main Menu bar, select **Edit.**
   or
   Press **Ctrl-Ins** and skip step 3.
3. From the Edit pull-down, select **Copy.**

• **NOTES** To copy data within the same 1-2-3 worksheet, use **Edit Quick Copy** instead. To both delete data from the current worksheet and to move it to the Clipboard in the same operation, use **Edit Cut.**

Copied data are retained on the Clipboard until you perform Edit Copy again or Edit Cut, either in 1-2-3 or in another Windows program. The Clipboard can be used to move data among 1-2-3 worksheets or among applications in Windows. (See "The Clipboard" in Part I.) To retrieve data from the Clipboard into the current 1-2-3 worksheet, use **Edit Paste.**

To copy worksheet files, see the corresponding File menu entries.

Edit Copy can also be used in conjunction with the Windows features of the Clipboard and Dynamic Data Exchange (DDE) to establish data links among Windows documents and applications. (See "The Clipboard" in Part I, "Edit Link Options," and "File Administration Update Links.")

See Also *Edit Cut, Edit Link Options, Edit Quick Copy, Edit Paste, File Administration Update Links, File Combine From, File Extract To, File Import From.* Part I: *The Clipboard.*

EDIT CUT

Permits you to both delete data from a highlighted cell or range in the current worksheet and also to move them to the Clipboard in a single operation. The data then can be retrieved to the current cell pointer location with the Edit Paste command.

To Cut Data to the Clipboard:

1. Highlight the cell or range from which data will be copied.
2. From the Main Menu bar, select **Edit.**
   or
   Press **Shift-Del** and skip step 3.
3. From the Edit pull-down, select **Cut.**

• NOTES To move data within the same worksheet, use **Edit Move Cells** instead. To delete data without involving the Clipboard, use **Edit Clear** or **Edit Clear Special.**

Data moved to the Clipboard with this command include text labels, numeric values, formulas, formatting, and graphs contained within the range you select in step 1.

Copied data are retained on the Clipboard until you perform Edit Copy or Edit Cut again, either in 1-2-3 or in another Windows program. The Clipboard can be used to move data among 1-2-3 worksheets or among applications in Windows. (See "The Clipboard" in Part I.) To retrieve data from the Clipboard into the current 1-2-3 worksheet, use **Edit Paste.**

See Also *Edit Clear, Edit Clear Special, Edit Copy, Edit Move Cells, Edit Paste.* Part I: *The Clipboard.*

EDIT FIND

Permits you to search for a specified string of characters in labels and/or formulas of a worksheet, or search for a string and replace it with another you specify.

To Search and/or Replace Strings:

1. If you wish, highlight a restricted search range.
2. From the Main Menu bar, select **Edit.**
3. From the Edit pull-down, select **Find.**
4. In the Search For text box, enter the string you wish to find.
5. Also in the dialog box, select one of the radio buttons, **Find** or **Replace With.**
6. If you selected Replace With in step 5, enter the replacement string in the Replace With text box.

7. Specify whether the search will look through labels, formulas, or both.
8. The range you selected in step 1 should appear in the Range field of the dialog box. If you wish, you can select a different range by entering a new range name or address here in the text box.
9. Select **Find Next.**
10. If found, the first occurrence of the string is highlighted in the worksheet. Select **Find Next** to find the next occurrence, or **Cancel** to end the search.

    or

    If you selected Replace With in step 5, the first occurrence of the string is highlighted in the worksheet. Select **Replace, Replace All, Next,** or **Cancel.**

• NOTES Edit Find cannot be used to search for data values. Searching is limited to alphanumeric text (labels) and formulas.

This command will find strings in cells for which the format is Hidden, but it will ignore hidden columns or worksheets that were marked with the Worksheet Hide command.

In step 6, the replacement string is limited to 512 characters.

• OPTIONS In the Edit Find dialog box in step 5, the options are Find, which only searches, or Replace With, which searches and replaces the found data with the string specified in the text box. In step 7, you can choose to search for strings in cells that only contain alphanumeric **Labels**, only contain **Formulas**, or **Both.**

See Also *Worksheet Hide.*

EDIT LINK OPTIONS

Establishes and maintains data links between the current worksheet and external files of other Windows applications. Links are managed under the Dynamic Data Exchange (DDE) feature of Windows, which passes data through the Clipboard. Changing the data at a linked location in one file will cause the data in the other to be updated. You can specify the type of data to be transferred, as well as whether the updating will be performed automatically or manually (using Edit Link Options Update or File Administration Update Links).

To Create a Data Link:

1. Start the application containing the information to be linked. Open the source file and select the desired data.
2. Copy the source data to the Clipboard by using **Edit Copy.**
3. Open the 1-2-3 worksheet file that will hold the linking data.
4. Highlight the cell or range that will serve as the *destination range.*
5. From the Main Menu bar, select **Edit.**
6. From the Edit pull-down, select **Link Options.**
7. In the Edit Link Options dialog box, select **Create.**
8. The Edit Link Options Create dialog box appears. If you wish to change the default link name assigned by the program, enter new information in the Link Name text box.
9. In the Format Name list box, select the data type or file format of the data to be transferred.
10. Select the **Automatic** or **Manual** Update Mode radio button.
11. If you wish to override the range selected in step 4, specify a range name or address in the Range text box.
12. In the Application text box, enter the name of the application program that will generate the source data.

    or

    From the list box, select one of the Windows applications currently open.

13. In the Topic Name text box, enter the file name (including its extension) that holds the source data.
    or
    From the list box, select one of the files currently open.
14. In the Item Name text box, enter the item, such as a field name, that holds the source data.
15. Select **OK.**
16. To return to the worksheet, select **Cancel.**

To Edit an Existing Data Link:

1. From the Main Menu bar, select **Edit.**
2. From the Edit pull-down, select **Link Options.**
3. The Edit Link Options dialog box appears, with all previously established link names in the Links list box. Select the name of the link to be edited.
4. Buttons in the dialog box now are undimmed, and current settings for the selected link appear in the Format information boxes. Select the **Edit** button.
5. The Edit Link Options Edit dialog box appears. Reset any of the options shown by performing steps 9–14 above.
6. Select **OK.**
7. To return to the worksheet, select **Cancel.**

To Maintain a Link:

1. From the Main Menu bar, select **Edit.**
2. From the Edit pull-down, select **Link Options.**
3. The Edit Link Options dialog box appears, with all previously established link names in the Links list box. Select the name of the link to be maintained.
4. Buttons in the dialog box now are undimmed, and current settings for the selected link appear in the Format information boxes. Select **Update** for a manual link to make data copies current in all files.

or

Select **Deactivate** to sever the link temporarily, until a link update is performed.

or

Select **Delete** to remove the link name you selected in step 3 and all its settings.

5. To return to the worksheet, select **Cancel.**

• NOTES In Windows DDE, the application that generates a source file is called a *server* and the destination program is called a *client.* Not all applications support DDE as both server and client. Check the program documentation to be sure. Lotus 1-2-3 for Windows supports both, so a worksheet file can be both a destination (receive data from an external source) and a source (send data to an external file). When you create a link with Edit Link Options Create, the current worksheet is the destination file and the external file is the source.

In some cases, data links need not be created explicitly with Edit Link Options. Links are also created when you use an external file reference in a worksheet formula (see "Formula Syntax") and when you use Edit Paste Link.

When using DDE, all linked files must be open. When files are linked with a formula, the file referenced in the formula can be closed and 1-2-3 will still perform the update.

• OPTIONS The following options appear in the Edit Link Options dialog box:

Create Settings are made in the Edit Link Options Create dialog box in step 8 of "To Create a Data Link." They include:

Link name Can be any text string. The program assigns the defaults LINK1, LINK2, and so on.

Format name Refers to the data type or file format of the data to be transferred. Options are TEXT (character data, the default), Lotus123Private (protected format), WK3 and WK1 (worksheet formats), METAFILEPICT (Computer Graphics Metafile format), DIB (Windows bitmap format), BITMAP (pixel array), and Lotus123Graph (graph data and formatting).

Update mode Must be either **Automatic** (an update in one file triggers the corresponding update in the other) or **Manual** (an update occurs only when you perform Edit Link Options Update or File Administration Update Links).

Application The name of any currently installed Windows application program that supports DDE.

Topic name The file name (including extension) that holds the source data.

Item name Refers to the record item or field in the source file. An item in an external worksheet might be a range address or name. In an external database field, the item might be a field name or search key. For files that have no such descriptors, enter a text string to serve as a label. If you try to leave this text box blank, an error message will appear.

Edit Brings up the Edit Link Options Edit dialog box. You can change any of the settings listed under Edit Link Options Create above, except the link name.

Update Updates the linked data item in both source and destination files, using the value currently in the source file.

Deactivate Severs the selected link until a link update is executed but retains the link name and settings in the list.

Delete Removes the selected link from the list of link names, along with its format settings.

See Also *Edit Copy, Edit Paste Link, File Administration Update Links, Formula Syntax.* Part I: *The Clipboard.*

EDIT MOVE CELLS

Permits you to move the contents of a highlighted cell or range to another location in any of the worksheets in the same file. Address references in formulas will be adjusted automatically by the program unless they have been specified as absolute with the $ syntax. (See "Range Addressing.")

To Move a Cell or Range:

1. Highlight the cell or range from which data will be copied.
2. From the Main Menu bar, select **Edit.**
3. From the Edit pull-down, select **Move Cells.**
4. In the Edit Move Cells dialog box, the range address you selected in step 1 appears in the From text box. Enter a new range address here to change it, if you wish.
5. In the To text box, enter the address of the first cell (top left).
6. To move only the formatting from the specified range, select the **Styles Only** check box.
7. Select **OK.**

• NOTES This command moves text labels, numeric values, formulas, cell formats, protection status, and formatting (styles). Data in the To range will be overwritten.

Edit Move Cells cannot operate among different files, and it does not pass data through the Clipboard. (See "The Clipboard" in Part I, as well as "Edit Cut" and "Edit Paste," for information about moving data among files and applications.)

To move data among worksheets in a three-dimensional file, precede the range address with the worksheet letter in step 5.

If the first cell in a named range is included in the From or To fields, the range definition will be changed. This also applies to a range that is referred to in formulas.

• OPTIONS If you select Styles Only in step 6, only the formatting is moved to the new location. (Formatting is done through the Styles menu.)

See Also *Edit Copy, Edit Cut, Edit Paste, Edit Quick Copy.*

EDIT PASTE

Retrieves data and formatting that was previously copied to the Clipboard area by an Edit Copy or Edit Cut command in 1-2-3 or another Windows application.

To Paste Data from the Clipboard:

1. Place data on the Clipboard with the **Edit Copy** or **Edit Cut** commands in 1-2-3 or another Windows application.
2. In 1-2-3, open the worksheet file that will receive the data.
3. Highlight the cell or range to which data will be copied.
4. From the Main Menu bar, select **Edit.**
   or
   Press **Shift-Ins** and skip step 5.
5. From the Edit pull-down, select **Paste.**

● **NOTES** To copy data within the same worksheet in 1-2-3, use **Edit Quick Copy** instead.

When data are copied to addresses that differ from those in the source file, the program updates the addresses, provided that the references are relative (the default) or mixed. The $ syntax can be used in addresses to specify that an address is absolute and can't be changed. (See "Range Addressing.")

Edit Paste can be performed repeatedly to retrieve multiple copies of the same source data, such as when you wish to place the data in different sheets in a three-dimensional file. Copied data are retained on the Clipboard until you perform Edit Copy or Edit Cut, either in 1-2-3 or in another Windows program. The Clipboard can be used to move data among 1-2-3 worksheets or among applications in Windows. (See "The Clipboard" in Part I.)

To copy worksheet files, see the corresponding File menu entries.

To establish a Dynamic Data Exchange (DDE) link between Windows files, use **Edit Paste Link** instead. (See "Edit Link Options," "Edit Paste Link," and "File Administration Update Links.")

See Also *Edit Cut, Edit Link Options, Edit Paste Link, Edit Quick Copy, File Administration Update Links, File Combine From, File Extract To, File Import From.* Part I: *The Clipboard.*

EDIT PASTE LINK

Copies data and formatting from the Clipboard to the current worksheet and also establishes a link to the source file from which the data were extracted. You can then perform Dynamic Data Exchange (DDE) among active Windows documents and applications. Changing the data in one application and file will change it in all the other active files to which it is linked.

To Paste Data and Link Files:

1. Place data on the Clipboard with the **Edit Copy** or **Edit Cut** commands in 1-2-3 or another Windows application.
2. In 1-2-3, open the worksheet file that will receive the data.
3. Highlight the cell or range to which data will be copied.
4. From the Main Menu bar, select **Edit.**
5. From the Edit pull-down, select **Paste Link.**

• **NOTES** If you are unable to establish a link using this command, use **Edit Link Options Create** and specify a DDE link.

All links to the current worksheet can be viewed in a list box by selecting **Edit Link Options.**

Formatting copied with Edit Paste includes settings made through the Style menu, such as Font and Color.

See Also *Edit Copy, Edit Cut, Edit Link Options, Edit Paste, Edit Quick Copy, File Combine From, File Extract To, File Import From.* Part I: *The Clipboard.*

EDIT QUICK COPY

Permits you to duplicate the highlighted cell or range at another location in the same or another worksheet in the same file. By default, text labels, numeric values, formulas, cell formats, formatting, and protection status are copied. You can choose to copy only styles (formatting) or to convert formulas to values.

To Copy Data and Formatting:

1. Highlight the cell or range from which data will be copied.
2. From the Main Menu bar, select **Edit.**
3. From the Edit pull-down, select **Quick Copy.**
4. In the Edit Quick Copy dialog box, the range address you selected in step 1 appears in the From text box. Enter a new range reference here to change it, if you wish.
5. In the To text box, enter the address of the first cell (top left) in the destination range.
6. To move only the formatting from the specified range, select the **Styles Only** check box.
7. To convert all formulas in the source range to numeric values in the destination range, select the **Convert to Values** check box.
8. Select **OK.**

• **NOTES** All data in the destination range are overwritten by this operation.

This command does not pass data through the Clipboard. To pass data among different Windows files and applications, use **Edit Copy** and **Edit Paste.**

To make multiple copies of a specified cell in a single step, select a cell in step 1 and enter a range in step 5. One copy will be placed in each cell of this range.

If you specify a three-dimensional range in step 1, be sure that the destination range includes at least as many sheets. Also, neither the source nor the destination ranges should extend beyond worksheet IV.

If you specify Convert to Values in step 7 and the CALC indicator is showing at the top right of the screen, select **Cancel**, press **F9** (Calc) to recalculate all formulas, then start again with step 1.

If the range you specify in step 1 contains any formulas that are linked to other files, first perform **File Administration Update Links** to be sure that all values are recalculated.

See Also *Edit Copy, Edit Move Cells, Edit Paste.*

EDIT UNDO

When this command is not dimmed in the Edit pull-down, selecting it will cancel the result of the most recent reversible command.

To Undo a Command:

1. *Before you execute another command,* from the Main Menu bar, select **Edit.**
   or
   Press **Alt-Backspace.**
2. From the Edit pull-down, select **Undo.**

• **NOTES** If the Undo selection is dimmed in the Edit pull-down, there is nothing in the command buffer (nothing to undo). When you perform Edit Undo, the item becomes dimmed, and the command cannot be reversed (you can't undo Edit Undo itself). You will not be able to complete Edit Undo if there is no more available memory.

Certain functions cannot be reversed, including F5 (Go To), F6 (Pane), and F9 (Calc). You also cannot undo the commands File Administration Update Links, File Save (As), or File Print.

See Also *Edit Clear, Edit Clear Special.*

ENTERING DATA

This is not a menu item but a description of the steps needed to enter data into a cell in the current worksheet.

To Enter Data

1. In the current worksheet window, use the mouse or the arrow keys to move to a blank cell that will hold the data.
2. The cell address appears in the *address box* near the top left corner of the 1-2-3 screen.
3. Key in the data. Enter numeric values directly. Precede labels (text) with a *label prefix.*
4. The data appear in the *contents box* to the right of the address box.
5. To accept the data as entered, click on the **Confirm** button (✓) to the left of the contents box, or press ↵.

   or

   To enter new data, select the **Cancel** button (X) to the left of the contents box, or press **Esc.**

or

To move to an adjacent cell to make another entry, press the appropriate arrow key (← ↓ ↑ →). Then press ↵ when you have made all entries in a range.

6. When you accept the data, your entry appears in the cell in the worksheet.

• OPTIONS Options for label prefixes in step 3 are the following: Align left ('); Align right ("); Align center (^); Fill cell with character (\); Omit print row if first cell in row, otherwise align left (|).

See Also *Formula Syntax.*

FILE ADMINISTRATION NETWORK RESERVE

Controls file sharing on network and multiuser systems. A reservation, a type of file lock, prevents access to a worksheet file while the user with the reservation is working with that file. At your option, the reservation can be assigned automatically for the duration of a work session to the first user who retrieves the file.

To Get or Release a File Reservation:

1. From the Main Menu bar, select **File.**
2. From the File pull-down, select **Administration.**
3. From the Administration cascade, select **Network Reserve.**
4. In the File Administration Network Reserve dialog box, select **Get** or **Release.**
5. Select **OK.**

• NOTES Assigning the reservation affects the file that is currently open in 1-2-3. You can select Get only if

- the file is available (not in use)

and

- the file hasn't been saved by someone else since you accessed it.

Once you have the reservation, you are the only user who can update the file.

To save changes you've made to a reserved file, save it before using the Release command to release its reservation.

• OPTION In step 4, to turn automatic file reservation on or off, select the **Get Reservation Automatically** check box. This check box, or toggle, is on when it is filled with an X. When the toggle is on, the file reservation is assigned to the first user who opens the file. Access by other users is restricted until the first user closes the file. (The toggle is on by default.)

FILE ADMINISTRATION PASTE TABLE

Creates a table that lists all active worksheet files and their data links, if any, to the current file. This table can be used as a basis for passing data among the files (using Edit Copy/Cut and Edit/Paste).

To Create a Paste Table:

1. Drag the pointer to select a range in the current worksheet to hold the paste table.
2. From the Main Menu bar, select **File.**
3. From the File pull-down, select **Administration.**

4. From the Administration cascade, select **Paste Table.**
5. In the File Administration Paste Table dialog box, select the radio button for **Active** or **Linked** files.
6. The range you selected in step 1 should appear in the Range field of the dialog box. If you wish, you can select a different range by entering a new range name or address here in the text box.
7. Select **OK.**

• NOTES In step 6, the table overwrites any existing data in the specified range. The table takes up one row for each file and a blank row.

• OPTIONS In step 5, radio buttons in the File Administration Paste Table dialog box correspond to the following options:

Active files Lists all open worksheet files (by row) with the data in columns for file name, date and time of last file update, size (bytes), number of worksheets containing data, modified (1) or unmodified (0), and file reserved for you (1) or file not reserved for you (0).

Linked files Lists all files (by row) that contain formulas linked to the current file. The columns in the table are file path and name, date and time of last update, and size (bytes).

See Also *Edit Link Options, Edit Paste Link, File Administration Network Reserve.*

FILE ADMINISTRATION SEAL FILE

Affects the usage of worksheet files that are shared in network and multiuser systems. With this command, you can seal, or lock, the settings and content of a shared worksheet file, as well as the reservation status assigned to it by a previous File Administration Network Reserve command.

To Seal a Shared File:

1. From the Main Menu bar, select **File.**
2. From the File pull-down, select **Administration.**
3. From the Administration cascade, select **Seal File.**
4. In the File Administration Seal File dialog box, select one of the radio buttons that control the extent of the change. (See "Options," below.)
5. Select **OK.**
6. If you selected the first option in step 4, the program will prompt you for a password to control file access. In the text boxes, key in a text string, reenter it to verify, and select **OK**.

• **NOTE** The reservation setting of a file is made with the File Administration Network Reserve command. When a file is sealed, this reservation setting cannot be changed until you explicitly remove all restrictions with the File Seal File Disable command (step 4 above). Some settings in the file relating to Graph, Range, Style, and Worksheet will be sealed also.

• **OPTIONS** In step 4 above, the following options appear as radio buttons in the File Administration Seal File dialog box, limiting changes to:

File and network reservation status Seals the current file content, as well as its reservation setting.

Reservation status only Seals only the setting made with File Administration Network Reserve.

Disable all restrictions Undoes a previous Seal command, unsealing both the file content and its reservation.

See Also *File Administration Network Reserve.*

FILE ADMINISTRATION UPDATE LINKS

Recalculates the formulas in all files linked to the current file. The effect is to update the results of all linked formulas. This command can be used while working on a worksheet. The links are also updated each time one of the linked files is opened.

To Update the Results of Linked Formulas:

1. From the Main Menu bar, select **File.**
2. From the File pull-down, select **Administration.**
3. From the Administration cascade, select **Update Links.**
4. To update the links automatically, set Tools User Setup Recalculation to **Automatic.**

   or

   Set the Tools User Setup Recalculation to **Manual** (the CALC indicator appears in the top right corner of the screen) and press **F9** (Calc) to update the links.

• **NOTE** Worksheet files in 1-2-3 for Windows can be linked in two ways. First, a formula in one file can include a reference to another file. A file reference within a formula is a file name enclosed in double angle brackets (<< >>). A path preceding the file name is optional. Files linked by formulas need not be open unless they are protected with passwords. A second method of linking files is through Dynamic Data Exchange (DDE). To use this feature of Windows, see "Edit Link Options" and "Edit Paste Link."

See Also *Edit Link Options, Edit Paste Link.*

FILE CLOSE

Closes the file indicated by the current position of the cell pointer.

To Close a File:

1. Move the cell pointer into the document window that contains the file you want to close.
2. From the Main Menu bar, select **File.**
3. From the File pull-down, select **Close.**
4. If the File Close dialog box appears, select **Yes** to save the file before closing, **No** to abandon the changes and close the file, or **Cancel** to keep the file open.

• **NOTE** Selecting Yes in step 4 is the same as executing File Save. The program will not warn you that the existing file is being overwritten. To rename the file as it is saved, use **File Save As** instead.

See Also *File Save, File Save As.*

FILE COMBINE FROM

Permits data and cell formats from a worksheet file on disk to be merged, or combined, with the current worksheet.

To Combine Worksheets:

1. In the current worksheet window, move the cell pointer to the location at which the merged data will appear.
2. From the Main Menu bar, select **File.**
3. From the File pull-down, select **Combine From.**

4. In the File Combine From dialog box, specify the file in the File name text box. (You can navigate disks and directories through the Files, Directories, and Drives boxes.)
5. Also in the dialog box, select one of the Action radio buttons and one of the Source buttons. (See "Options," below.)
6. If you selected Range in step 4, specify a range name or address in the Range text box. This range is the location in the source file of the desired data.
7. Select **OK.**

• NOTES If the file you specify in step 4 is protected, the program will prompt you for a password.

Settings in the current worksheet are used for worksheet settings, column widths, and range names for the merged data.

Data are inserted in the worksheet at the location of the current cell, which will correspond to the top left cell in the imported range.

Unless the Add or Subtract options are set, merged data will overwrite any data at the point of insertion. To avoid losing data in a worksheet, save the prior version first before executing this command.

Avoid combining formulas with three-dimensional ranges into a file that does not have at least the same number of worksheets.

If you select the Add or Subtract options for Actions in step 5, don't include dates or times in the values.

• OPTIONS The following options must be set in the File Combine From dialog box in steps 5 and 6.

Action One of the following radio buttons must be selected to specify the file merge action:

Copy Makes a copy of the data in the source file and inserts it at the cell pointer location in the current worksheet.

Add Adds any numeric values in the source worksheet to numeric values or blanks in the current worksheet. Labels and formulas in the current worksheet are retained, and source data that might overwrite them are discarded.

Subtract Subtracts the source numeric data from the numeric values in the current worksheet. Labels and formulas in the current worksheet are retained, and source data that might overwrite them are discarded. Blanks in the current worksheet are interpreted as zeros, resulting in negative values after subtraction.

Source Select one of the following options relating to the source worksheet file:

Entire file Merges all the data from the specified file.

Range Merges only the range specified in the accompanying text box.

FILE EXIT

Ends a 1-2-3 work session, quits the program, and returns you to the Lotus Applications window of Windows Program Manager.

To Exit 1-2-3:

1. From the Main Menu bar, select **File.**
   or
   Double-click on the Control box in the top left corner of the 1-2-3 window. Skip step 2.
2. From the File pull-down, select **Exit.**
3. In the File Exit dialog box, select **Yes** to save the current worksheet to disk before exiting, **No** to abandon the worksheet changes and exit, or **Cancel** to return to 1-2-3.

FILE EXTRACT TO

Permits you to copy data and/or formulas from the currently highlighted cell or range to another file on disk.

To Extract Data to a File:

1. In the current worksheet window, highlight a range of data to be extracted.
2. From the Main Menu bar, select **File.**
3. From the File pull-down, select **Extract To.**
4. In the File Extract To dialog box, specify the file in the File name text box. (You can navigate disks and directories through the Files, Directories, and Drives boxes.)
5. Also in the dialog box, select one of the Save As radio buttons. (See "Options," below.)
6. If you wish to override the range selected in step 1, specify a range name or address in the Range text box.
7. Select **OK.**

• **NOTES** If you specify an existing file in step 4, the program prompts you to cancel the command, replace the data, or create a backup of the file before overwriting its data.

Data cannot be extracted from a sealed file. Release any file reservation before executing this command.

A Release 2 file cannot be created from the current .WK3 file if it contains multiple worksheets. (You can't extract three-dimensional information to a two-dimensional file.)

Make sure that all references in formulas and range names are included in the range to be extracted. If the CALC indicator is showing in the top right corner of the screen, press **F9** (Calc) to recalculate the formulas before executing this command.

Make sure links to multiple files have been updated before executing this command. (See "File Administration Update Links.")

• **OPTIONS** In the File Extract To dialog box in step 5, use Save As to save the data and/or formulas in the indicated range in one of the following formats:

Formulas Copies both data and any accompanying formulas from the current worksheet to the target file.

Values Converts formulas to values and copies them, along with data in the specified range, to the target file.

FILE IMPORT FROM

Permits you to bring data, as well as styles such as fonts and graphics, into the current worksheet from other data files. Source file formats can include text (delimited or not), 1-2-3 Format, Impress, or Allways.

To Import Data or Styles:

1. Move the cell pointer to the location in the current worksheet where the imported data will be inserted.
2. From the Main Menu bar, select **File.**
3. From the File pull-down, select **Import From.**
4. From the Import From cascade, select **Text, Numbers,** or **Styles.** (See "Options," below.)
5. In the File Import dialog box, specify the name of the external file in the File name text box. (You can navigate disks and directories through the Files, Directories, and Drives boxes.)
6. If you selected Styles in step 4, select one of the Import radio buttons in the dialog box. (See "Options," below.)
7. Select **OK.**

• NOTES To avoid losing data, save your work before executing this command.

When using either the Text or Numbers options, decimal points are permitted in data items in the source file but commas (which would be interpreted as delimiters) are not accepted.

If labels are too long after the data are imported, use the **Data Parse** command to break up a label among multiple cells in the worksheet.

When using the Style option, formats are imported to match their positions in the source file. Ideally, the layouts of the two files should match. To change the locations of imported formats, use **Edit Move Cells.**

When graphs from 1-2-3 are imported, they act as templates. Only their positions and enhancements are imported, not their data. This template can therefore be used to control the style of graphed data in the current worksheet.

• OPTIONS The following options appear in the cascade menu in step 4. Selecting one of these brings up a dialog box for specifying the file and, in the case of Style, for specifying import options.

Text Imports alphanumeric data from a file that is not delimited (contains no commas or other delimiters between fields). Each line of data in the source file is inserted in a cell of the current worksheet as a long label, proceeding downward in the same column. Labels longer than 512 characters will be truncated.

Numbers Imports alphanumeric data from a *delimited* text file. An example would be the record

"Evan Jones",123,"Main Street","Anytown","USA"

Text fields are imported as labels and numeric data as values. Each field is inserted in a cell of the current worksheet. If this option is used with a text file that is not delimited, only the numeric values will be imported.

Style Imports user-named styles (through the Style menu), font sets, or graphics from files in the following formats: 1-2-3 (.FM3), Impress (.FMT), or Allways (.ALL).

All From the external format file, replaces all named styles, formats, fonts, and graphics.

Named styles Makes the current file match only the named styles in the external file.

Fonts Makes the fonts in the current file match those in the external file.

Graphics Copies graphics in the external file to the current file, including their positions and enhancements, but retains any graphics already in the current file.

FILE NEW

Opens a new worksheet file and displays it as a blank document window in 1-2-3.

To Open a New Worksheet File:

1. From the Main Menu bar, select **File.**
2. From the File pull-down, select **New.**
3. A blank document window appears, with the cell pointer at location A1. Enter your data.

• NOTES The program automatically assigns a name to the file, which appears in the title bar of its document window. The default name is FILE*N*.WK3, where *N* is the consecutive number of new sheets (001–256).

To change the default file name, save and close the file with **File Save As.** If you wish, you can also assign a password to the file during this operation.

To accept the default file name when you save the file, simply choose **File Save.**

See Also *File Open, File Save, File Save As.*

FILE OPEN

Loads an existing worksheet file from disk to become the current worksheet in 1-2-3.

To Open a Worksheet File:

1. From the Main Menu bar, select **File.**
2. From the File pull-down, select **Open.**
3. In the File Open dialog box, specify the file in the File name text box. (You can navigate disks and directories through the Files, Directories, and Drives boxes.)
4. Select **OK.**
5. The contents of the file appear in a new document window in 1-2-3. The cell pointer is active within the new window.

• **NOTE** Multiple files can be loaded into 1-2-3 concurrently. Their document windows will overlay one another on the screen. To move the cell pointer among them, simply click on the title bar of the window you want. Or, press **Ctrl-F6** to cycle through the open document windows.

FILE PAGE SETUP

Brings up a dialog box in which you can specify the layout and organization of printed worksheet pages, including headers and footers.

To Specify Page Setup:

1. From the Main Menu bar, select **File.**

2. From the File pull-down, select **Page Setup.**
3. In the File Page Setup dialog box, enter text in the Header and Footer fields, if you wish.
4. Also in the dialog box, change any of the default options settings to control the look of the page. (See "Options," below.)
5. Select **OK.**

• NOTES The Landscape option will work only on printers that support this mode. That is, the program will not rotate the output to produce Landscape orientation on a Portrait printer. However, this *is* a feature of some add-in programs, such as Allways.

If you find yourself frequently resetting the page appearance options, save the settings to a page layout library file. (See "Named Settings," below.)

• OPTIONS Page Setup options appear in the dialog box in steps 3 and 4.

Header and Footer Enter text strings to be printed as header and footer on the top and bottom of each page. Leaving these fields blank clears the existing headers or footers.

Margins Enter new margins as measurements on the output page for the top, bottom, left, and right dimensions. Default settings are shown for the output format used with the currently installed printer.

Borders Determines which portion of the worksheet will appear on the printed page. The Columns setting determines the leftmost column of each page and print range. The Rows setting establishes the top of the page, which is above the print range.

Compression Squeezes or expands, in effect, a worksheet to fit the print area. Select one of the following radio buttons:

Automatically fit to page Adjusts the degree of compression according to the Margins and Borders settings.

Manually size Reduces or enlarges the worksheet by the percentage you specify. For example, an entry of 150 would enlarge the worksheet 1.5 times.

None Performs no compression or enlargement.

Options Set any of the following toggles to control the appearance of the page (X = on, blank = off).

Show formulas Prints the formula in any cell instead of its data value.

Show worksheet frame Draws a frame around the page.

Show grid lines Separates columns and rows with grid lines.

Orientation Select **Landscape** (long dimension is horizontal) or **Portrait** (long dimension is vertical).

Default Settings To return options to their default settings, select **Restore.** To change the defaults to the current, revised settings so that they affect future sessions, select **Update.**

Named Settings To save settings in this dialog box to a page layout library file, select **Save** and specify the file name. The extension is .AL3. To retrieve an existing page layout and reset the current dialog box, select **Retrieve** and specify the file.

See Also *File Preview.*

FILE PREVIEW

Displays a simulation of printed worksheet outputs on your computer screen. If included in the worksheet, margins, frames, grids, styles (such as graphics), and attributes (such as fonts) will be shown, sized and positioned correctly in relation to the output page.

To Preview Printed Pages:

1. Highlight the ranges in the current worksheet that you want to print.
2. From the Main Menu bar, select **File.**
3. From the File pull-down, select **Preview.**
4. In the File Preview dialog box, you can specify one or more print ranges in the Range(s) text box. (Use semi-colons (;) to separate multiple range addresses or names.)
5. Also in the dialog box, specify which pages are to be previewed.
6. If you wish to change the appearance of the page before you preview it, select the **Page Setup** button and reset the File Page Setup dialog box. (See "File Page Setup.")
7. Select **OK.**
8. The first printed page appears on the screen. To cycle through multiple pages, press **Esc** repeatedly.
9. When you have viewed the last page, press **Esc** again to return to the worksheet document window.

• NOTE Selecting the Page Setup button in step 6 is the same as executing the File Page Setup command and takes you to a dialog box for entry of the header and footer, as well as options for the layout and appearance of the printed page. See the "Options" section of the entry "File Page Setup."

• OPTIONS In step 5, specify the starting page in the From Page text box and the ending page in the To box. To renumber the first page in the print range, enter the page number in the Starting Page Number box.

See Also *File Page Setup.*

FILE PRINT

Outputs the current worksheet file to the printer.

To Print a File:

1. Highlight the ranges in the current worksheet that you want to print.
2. From the Main Menu bar, select **File.**
3. From the File pull-down, select **Print.**
4. In the File Print dialog box, you can specify one or more print ranges in the Range(s) text box. (Use semicolons (;) to separate multiple range addresses or names.)
5. Also in the dialog box, specify which pages are to be printed.
6. If you wish to change the appearance of the page before you print it, select the **Page Setup** button and reset the File Page Setup dialog box. (See "File Page Setup.")
7. Before printing, to see how pages will look, select the **Preview** button. (See "File Preview.")
8. Select **OK.**

• NOTES In the File Print dialog box in steps 6 and 7, selecting Page Setup is the same as executing the File Page Setup command, presenting you with a dialog box for headers, footers, and page appearance options. Selecting Preview is the same as executing File Preview, displaying an on-screen simulation of each page in the print range.

If a print range includes a long label, include the overlapped cells as well as the cell that holds the label in steps 1 and 4.

• OPTIONS In step 5, specify in the Number of Copies text box how many times the file is to be printed. Also specify the starting page in the From Page text box and the ending page in the To box. To renumber the first page in the print range, enter the page number in the Starting Page Number box.

See Also *File Page Setup, File Preview.*

FILE PRINTER SETUP

Permits you to change options for a printer already installed.

To Set Printer Options:

1. From the Main Menu, select **File.**
2. From the File pull-down, select **Printer Setup.**
3. In the File Printer Setup dialog box, select the printer name in the Printer list box.
4. To accept the default options for the printer you've selected, select the **OK** button.
   or
   To change the options, select the **Setup** button.
5. A dialog box containing options for the installed printer appears. Reset the options shown. (See "Options," below.)
6. Select **OK.**

• **NOTES** Printers shown in the list box in step 3 must have been installed previously through the Windows Program Manager Control Panel. When you change settings with this command, you're actually making the changes in Windows.

To install a different printer, exit to Program Manager and select **Add Printer** from the Printers dialog box of the Control Panel (found in the Main program group).

• **OPTIONS** Options in the printers configure setup dialog box (these vary among the printer driver families, or subgroups by make and model) include the following:

Printer Select the specific model number of your printer from the printer driver family. (As an alternative, choose an emulation in another printer driver family.)

Graphic resolution Typical options include High, Medium, and Low.

Orientation Select **Landscape** (long dimension is horizontal) or **Portrait** (long dimension is vertical).

Paper source The options available may include Manual feed, Tractor feed, and Sheet feed (Bin 1 or Bin 2).

Paper size Select among the paper sizes your printer supports, which can include Letter, Legal, Wide (14 x 11 inches), A4 (European letter size), Fanfold, and A3.

Fonts If the printer supports multiple fonts, select the **Font** button in the dialog box and then select the desired font from the Font Options list box.

See Also *File Page Setup, File Preview, File Print.*

FILE SAVE

Writes the current worksheet to disk with the file name shown in the title bar of the worksheet's document window.

To Save a File:

1. Move the cell pointer into the document window of the worksheet you want to save.
2. From the Main Menu bar, select **File.**
3. From the File pull-down, select **Save.**

• NOTES The program will not warn you if this action will overwrite an existing file.

To rename the file when it is saved, use **File Save As** instead.

See Also *File Save As.*

FILE SAVE AS

Permits you to rename the current worksheet file as it is saved to disk. Optionally, you can specify password protection for the new file.

To Rename and Save a File:

1. Move the cell pointer into the document window of the worksheet you want to save.
2. From the Main Menu bar, select **File.**
3. From the File pull-down, select **Save As.**
4. In the File Save As dialog box, specify the new file name in the File Name text box. (You can navigate disks and directories through the Files, Directories, and Drives boxes.)
5. Also in the dialog box, select the Password Protect toggle if you wish to restrict access to the file.
6. To save all files that are currently active, select **Save All.**
7. Select **OK.**

• NOTES To save the current worksheet file without renaming it, use **File Save** instead. The file name is shown in the title bar of its document window.

If you specify an existing file in step 4, the program prompts you to cancel the command, replace the data, or create a backup of the file before overwriting its data.

If you turn on password protection in step 5, the program will prompt you for a password.

Password protection cannot be chosen if you select Save All in step 6. Save All causes all active files that have been modified to be saved to disk. To delete a password, turn the toggle off in step 5. To change a password, delete it, then turn the toggle back on, repeating step 5 and entering a new password.

See Also *File Save.*

FORMULA SYNTAX

In 1-2-3, a *formula* is a set of calculations containing variables that result in a single data value. Variables can include cell and range addresses, as well as range names. Calculations contained in formulas can include arithmetic operations, logical operations, and @functions. In 1-2-3, @functions are keywords that stand for predefined formulas (see Part IV).

To Enter a Formula into a Worksheet:

1. In the current worksheet window, move the cell pointer to a blank cell that will hold the formula.
2. The cell address appears in the Address box near the top left corner of the 1-2-3 screen.
3. Key in the formula. If the formula begins with a cell address or text string, precede it with a plus sign (+). To make the result of the formula negative, precede it instead with a minus sign (–).
4. The formula appears in the Contents box to the right of the Address box. (See Figure II.7.)

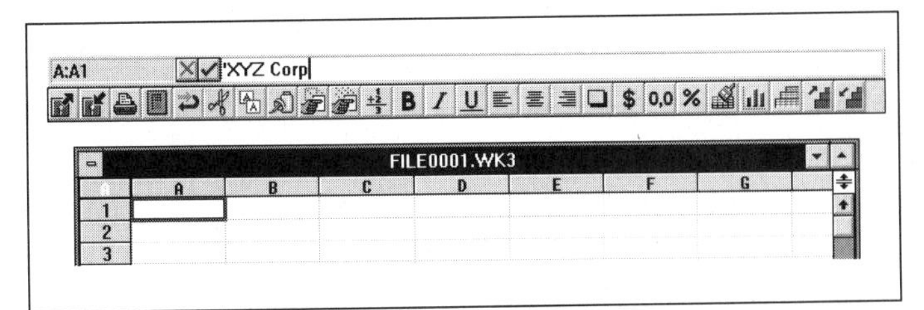

Figure II.7: The Contents box near the top left corner of the 1-2-3 screen shows data entries as you key them in. Select the X button to cancel or the ✓ button to confirm an entry.

5. To accept the formula as entered, click on the **Confirm** button (✓) to the left of the Contents box, or press ↵.

   or

   To enter a new formula, select the **Cancel** button (X) to the left of the Contents box, or press **Esc.**

   or

   To move to an adjacent cell to make another entry, press the appropriate arrow key (← ↓ ↑ →). Then press ↵ when you have made all entries in a range.

6. When you accept the formula, its result appears in the cell in the worksheet.

• **NOTES** Cell addresses in formulas can be relative, absolute, or mixed (see "Range Addressing"). However, when a range name is used in a formula, its range definition must include either relative *or* absolute addresses; they cannot be mixed. The program automatically adjusts relative addresses to allow for your insertions, deletions, moving, or copying of cells.

Do not include spaces within formulas. If you have entered a formula incorrectly or it refers to an invalid address, **ERR** is displayed in its cell.

When they are calculated, formulas are evaluated in left-to-right order. Also, certain kinds of operations will precede others. Arithmetic operations are evaluated first (multiplication and division are done before addition and subtraction), then logical operations, then string concatenation. As in arithmetic, the order of evaluation can be changed by enclosing items to be evaluated first in parentheses. Multiple pairs of parentheses, or nested formulas, are permissible.

A formula in one worksheet can include a reference to another file creating a link to the external file. A file reference within a formula is a file name enclosed in double angle brackets (<< >>). A path preceding the file name is optional. This file reference normally would proceed a range reference (address or name) in a formula.

• OPTIONS Formulas are of three general types:

Numeric Formulas Numeric formulas result in numbers. They contain arithmetic operations and @functions that result in numbers, dates, or times. Arithmetic operators, in order of precedence, are:

^(exponentiation)

+ or – (signed values)

* (multiplication)

/ (division)

+ (addition)

– (subtraction)

Logical Formulas Logical formulas use the logical operators (in order of precedence: =, <, ≤, >,≥ , <>, #AND#, #OR#, #NOT#) in statements that result in either True or False. If True, **1** is displayed in the cell. If the result is False, **0** is displayed.

String Formulas A string formula operates on labels, or text strings. (Label data contained in cells must be preceded by label prefixes. See "Entering Data.") String formulas concatenate, or combine by stringing together, cell addresses that contain labels. A string formula uses the operator & to indicate concatenation. Literal strings, or label constants, can be inserted in string formulas by enclosing them in quotation marks (" "). For example, the string formula +A1&B1&" USA" would cause the labels in cells A1 and B1 to be concatenated with the literal string **USA**.

See Also *Entering Data, Range Addressing. Part IV: @Functions.*

FUNCTION KEYS

Keys labeled F1–F10 on the keyboard perform specific program operations, or functions. Function-key assignments are listed on the inside back cover of this book. Keys F11 and F12 are not used in 1-2-3. Function keys can cause other actions when used in combination with Ctrl or Alt keys. These key combinations in 1-2-3 are called *accelerator keys*. (Do not confuse function keys with @functions, which are the names of predefined formulas. For more information about @functions, see Part IV.)

RANGE ADDRESSING

This entry is not a menu item. Rather, it describes how cells and ranges can be referenced in 1-2-3 commands and formulas.

A range is a rectangular block of contiguous cells. A range can be specified by two cell addresses: the cell in its top left corner (see Figure II.8) and the cell in its bottom right corner. If the range includes only a single column, its boundaries are the top and bottom cells. If the range includes just one row, its boundaries are the cells at its left and right ends. A range can also be a single cell, in which case its address is simply the cell address.

To Key in a Range Address:

1. When you see a text box labeled **Range** within a dialog box, click on the text box to activate its cursor. Or, press **Tab** repeatedly until the box is highlighted.
2. Key in the range address, using the syntax *W:Am..X:Zn.* (See "Notes," below.)

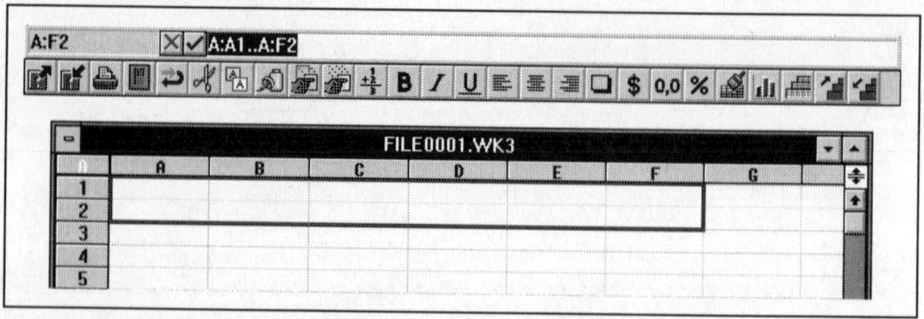

Figure II.8: The Address box near the top left corner of the 1-2-3 screen shows the cell address corresponding to the current location of the cell pointer; in this case, a highlighted range

To Specify a Range with the Mouse:

1. Move the cell pointer to the worksheet that contains the range to be selected.
2. Move the cell pointer to the cell in the first (top left) corner in the range.
3. Drag the pointer to the opposite corner and release. The entire range should now be highlighted.

To Specify a Range by Name:

1. Drag the cell pointer to highlight the desired range.
2. Use **Range Name Create** or **Range Name Label Create** to assign a name to the range you have specified.
3. Whenever the program prompts you for a range address (as in a text box labeled **Range**), simply enter the name instead.

• NOTES When you enter a range address from the keyboard in step 2, the syntax is

W Letter of the top worksheet in a three-dimensional range (optional).

A Column letter of the cell in the first (top left) corner.

m Row number of the cell in the first corner.

X Letter of the bottom worksheet in a three-dimensional range (optional).

Z Column letter of the cell in the second (bottom right) corner.

n Row number of the second corner.

The *W* and *X* parameters are used for specifying three-dimensional ranges, which can span multiple sheets in the same file. The worksheet letter must be separated from the cell address by a colon (:). To specify a range within the current worksheet, you must omit *both* worksheet letters from the syntax. That is, *Am..Zn* is interpreted as a range in the current worksheet. In any range address, the first and second cell addresses must be separated by the double-period (..) symbol and must not contain any spaces (blanks).

• OPTIONS In 1-2-3, references to cell addresses normally are adjusted when columns, rows, or ranges are inserted or deleted. However, syntax options make it possible to control the ways in which addresses are adjusted.

Relative By default, addresses are relative; they are adjusted by the program automatically. Addresses that can be changed include references in formulas and range name definitions. To specify relative addressing, simply use the syntax described above.

Absolute Any element of a range or cell address (sheet letter, column letter, and/or row number) can be specified as absolute, or fixed, by preceding it with a dollar sign ($) in the address syntax. Examples include $A$1, $A$1..$ZZ$99, and $A:$A$1..$ZZ:$ZZ$99.

Mixed In some circumstances, it might be necessary to specify one corner of a range as fixed and the other as relative. Thus, a range address can be mixed, or include both relative and absolute references. Examples include A$1 (column relative, row absolute) $A$1..ZZ99 (first corner absolute, second corner relative).

See Also *Range Name.*

RANGE ANNOTATE

Permits you to add annotations, including text, graphs, and drawings, to a specified range.

To Annotate a Range:

1. In the current worksheet window, move the cell pointer to highlight a range to be annotated.
2. From the Main Menu bar, select **Range.**
3. From the Range pull-down, select **Annotate.**
4. The Range Annotate dialog box appears. If you wish to override the range selected in step 1, specify a range name or address in the Range text box.
5. Select **OK.**
6. A new document window appears to hold the annotation. The Graph icon palette appears. Select text, graph, or drawing icons from the palette to create annotations in the document window. (See Part III: "The Graph Window Menu.")
7. Close or minimize the annotation document window.
8. To retain the annotation, use **File Save** to save the worksheet file.

• NOTES Annotations are documents associated with a worksheet file as graphs. To view an annotation, move the cell pointer to the range that contains it and use **Graph View.**

See Also *Graph Create, Graph Name, Graph View.*

RANGE FORMAT

Sets various parameters that affect the display of the current range and its values. These settings apply only to the specified range and override Worksheet Global Settings.

To Set Range Format:

1. In the current worksheet window, highlight a range to be formatted.
2. From the Main Menu bar, select **Range.**
3. From the Worksheet pull-down, select **Format.**
4. In the Range Format dialog box, make selections for the options Format, Decimal Places, and Parentheses.
   or
   To return to format defaults, select **Reset.**
5. If you wish to override the range selected in step 1, specify a range name or address in the Range text box.
6. Select **OK.**

• NOTES If you specify anything other than General in Format options, you must also make an entry in the Decimal Places text box.

If you select Reset in step 4, the Worksheet Global Settings are used.

If you specify a format that is too wide for the corresponding column width, the cell is displayed filled with asterisks (*********) instead of the value. (See "Worksheet Column Width.")

• OPTIONS Options in the dialog box in step 4 include the following:

Format

Fixed Truncates values to the specified number of decimal places.

Scientific Displays in exponential notation (power of 10).

Currency Shows with currency sign and decimal point.

,(Comma) Shows with thousands separator.

General Shows numbers without thousands separator (the default).

+/– In place of the value, shows a bar graph of plus or minus signs equivalent to the integral value.

Percent Displays with a trailing % sign.

Text Shows formulas as text, numbers as General.

Hidden Hides; does not display or print.

Automatic Lets the program determine best fit.

Label Adds the label prefix (′) automatically to any data entered here.

Numbered date and time formats 1–9 Selects from a variety of date and time formats.

Parentheses Encloses minus values in parentheses ().

Decimal Places Enter a value from 1–15 for the number of digits to appear to the right of the decimal point.

See Also *Range Unprotect, Worksheet Column Width, Worksheet Global Settings.*

RANGE GO TO

Causes the cell pointer to jump to the first cell in the range you specify by address or name.

To Go To a Range:

1. From the Main Menu bar, select **Range.**
   or
   Press **F5** (Go To) and skip step 2.
2. From the Range pull-down, select **Go To.**

3. In the Range Go To dialog box, enter a range name or address in the Range text box.
   or
   Select a range name from the list box.

4. Select **OK.** The cell pointer moves to the specified location in the current worksheet.

• NOTES Use **Go To** to move the cell pointer into a hidden range when the program is in READY mode. (See "Worksheet Hide.")

Range names will appear in the list box in step 3 only if range names have been defined previously through Range Name Create or Range Name Label Create.

To move the cell pointer to another worksheet file that is currently open, include the path and file name in the entry in step 3. Enclose the path and file name in double angle brackets (<<>>). It must precede the range address.

See Also *Range Name Create, Range Name Label Create, Worksheet Hide.*

RANGE JUSTIFY

Enables you to fit a column of labels within a specified column width. The text will be shrunk so that the longest label fits within the column.

To Justify a Range:

1. In the current worksheet window, from the top of the column that contains the labels, highlight a range of across which labels will be justified. Omit step 4.
   or
   Move the cell pointer to the top cell in the column to be justified, and enter a range in step 4.

2. From the Main Menu bar, select **Range.**
3. From the Range pull-down, select **Justify.**
4. In the Range Justify dialog box, specify a range name or address in the Range text box.
5. Select **OK.**

• NOTES For purposes of using this command, labels must be in a single column that contains only labels (no blanks or numeric values). The justification range can be a group of adjacent columns across which the labels will be justified. The width is the combined width of the columns in the justification range.

If you select the justification range in step 1, the Range Justify dialog box will not appear.

Protection must be off in Worksheet Global Settings for this command to operate.

The program left-aligns the labels and assigns the format and protection status of the first cell in the label column. If the justification range contains a single row, labels will be spread across it. The program may move adjacent data cells down to accommodate the labels.

See Also *Worksheet Column Width, Worksheet Global Settings.*

RANGE NAME CREATE/DELETE

Permit you to create or delete the name of a selected range address. (A *range* is a block of contiguous cells. A range address that is associated with a name is a *range name definition.*) Range names can be used instead of addresses in formulas and in any text box that requires a range entry.

To Create a Range Name:

1. In the current worksheet window, highlight a range of cells to be named.
2. From the Main Menu bar, select **Range.**
3. From the Range pull-down, select **Name.**
4. From the Range Name cascade, select **Create.**
5. In the Range Name Create dialog box, enter a name (1–15 characters) in the Name text box.
   or
   To include the selected range in the definition of an existing range name, select a name from the list box, and enter the new range definition in step 6.
6. If you wish to override the range selected in step 1, specify a range name or address in the Range text box. (If you select an existing name from the list box, its address appears here.)
7. Select the **Create** button.
8. Create more range names by repeating steps 5–7.
9. Select **OK.**

To Delete a Range Name:

1. From the Main Menu bar, select **Range.**
2. From the Range pull-down, select **Name.**
3. From the Range Name cascade, select **Delete.**
4. In the Range Name Delete dialog box, enter a name (1–15 characters) to be deleted in the Name text box.
   or
   Select a name from the list box.
5. Select the **Delete** button to delete the name.
   or
   Select the **Undefine** button to disassociate the name from its range address.

or

Select **Delete All** to delete all previously defined names in the current worksheet file.

6. To delete or undefine other range names, repeat steps 4 and 5.

7. Select **OK.**

• NOTES Use step 6 to create multiple range names, particularly if you want to define a three-dimensional range. (See "Range Addressing.") To place the range name into the worksheet as a visible label, create the name with this command, then use **Range Name Label Create.**

For a single-cell range address in a formula to be replaced automatically with the name you create here, the address must be expressed as a range. For example, use A1..A1 rather than A1. When you delete a range name, the program replaces it in all formulas with the range address.

To make a range name refer to an absolute (fixed) address, precede the name with a dollar ($) sign.

In general, no spaces, punctuation, or special characters are permitted in range names. Avoid names that look like addresses, formulas, keywords, macro commands, etc.

If you use Undefine with a range name that is used in a formula, the result will be displayed as **ERR**.

See Also *Range Name Label Create.*

RANGE NAME LABEL CREATE

Assigns a label to a single-cell range by taking existing label text from adjacent cells.

To Create a Range Name Label:

1. In the current worksheet window, highlight one cell to which the range name label will be assigned.
2. From the Main Menu bar, select **Range.**
3. From the Range pull-down, select **Name.**
4. From the Range Name cascade, select **Label Create.**
5. In the Range Name Label Create dialog box, select the position of the cell or cells containing the label, relative to the cell selected in step 1.
6. If you wish to use labels from a range that is not adjacent to the selected cell, specify the range name or address in the Range text box.
7. Select **OK.**

• NOTES This feature is a convenient shortcut for naming ranges, since labels that define ranges may already exist in the worksheet as captions, column headings, and so on.

Unless you specify a range explicitly in step 6, the range that holds the labels must touch the selected cell.

The program will substitute the name you create with this command in any formulas that refer to its range. For a single-cell range address in a formula to be replaced automatically with the name you create here, the address must be expressed as a range. For example, use A1..A1 rather than A1.

Labels must be the same length as range names (1–15 characters).

• OPTIONS In the dialog box in step 5, radio buttons appear for the following options, corresponding to the position of the label text in the worksheet in relation to the cell to be named: Left, Right, Up, and Down.

See Also *Range Name Create.*

RANGE NAME PASTE TABLE

Inserts a table of range names and their addresses that are associated with the current file into the current worksheet.

To Paste a Table of Range Names:

1. In the current worksheet window, highlight a range to hold the table.
2. From the Main Menu bar, select **Range.**
3. From the Range pull-down, select **Name.**
4. From the Range Name cascade, select **Paste Table.**
5. If you did not select a range in step 1 or selected only a single cell, the Range Name Paste Table dialog box appears. Specify a range name or address in the Range text box. (The first cell address is sufficient.)
6. Select **OK.**

• NOTES The range name table is composed of labels in two columns. The first column lists each range name in alphabetical order, and the second column lists the corresponding range address. The table overwrites any data in the selected range.

See Also *Range Addressing.*

RANGE PROTECT/UNPROTECT

Range Unprotect permits you to remove protection (read-only status) from a selected range in a globally protected worksheet file. The Range Protect command can be used only to reverse a previous Range Unprotect command.

To Protect or Unprotect a Range:

1. In the current worksheet window, highlight a range for which protection status will be changed.
2. From the Main Menu bar, select **Range.**
3. From the Range pull-down, select **Protect** (make read-only) or **Unprotect** (remove protection).
4. If you did not select a range in step 1 or selected only a single cell, a dialog box appears. Specify a range name or address in the Range text box.
5. Select **OK.**

• **NOTES** The symbol **PR** appears in the format line of a protected cell, **U** for an explicitly unprotected cell. Range Protect operates only on ranges that have been unprotected (Range Unprotect) in a worksheet file that has Worksheet Global Settings Protection turned on.

See Also *Worksheet Global Settings.*

RANGE TRANSPOSE

Copies data from one range to another. In the process, the arrangement of the data is transposed (horizontal to vertical or vertical to horizontal), and all formulas are converted to values.

To Copy and Transpose Data:

1. Be sure all formula calculations and data links are updated. (See "Notes," below.)
2. In the current worksheet window, highlight a range of data to be transposed.
3. From the Main Menu bar, select **Range.**
4. From the Range pull-down, select **Transpose.**
5. The Range Transpose dialog box appears. If you wish to override the range selected in step 1, specify a range name or address in the From text box.
6. Enter the destination range in the To text box. (The address of the first cell is sufficient.)
7. Select **OK.**
8. If you specified three-dimensional ranges in steps 5 or 6, the Range Transpose Options dialog box appears. Select options and then **OK.**

• NOTES Transposing data causes columns to be converted to rows, and vice versa. Addresses are adjusted accordingly.

If you specify a three-dimensional range in the From text box, there should be at least the same number of sheets in the To range.

• OPTIONS For three-dimensional transpositions, selections in the dialog box in step 8 are the following:

Rows/Columns Transposes rows (horizontally arranged data) so they become columns within each worksheet.

Columns/Worksheets Copies each column in the From range in sequence to become a row in a different worksheet in the To range.

Worksheets/Rows Copies each row from each worksheet in the From range in sequence to become a column in a different worksheet in the To range.

See Also *Edit Copy, Edit Move Cells, Edit Quick Copy.*

STYLE ALIGNMENT

Permits you to override the label alignment, or justification, specified in Worksheet Global Settings for a selected range.

To Align Labels in a Range:

1. In the current worksheet window, highlight a range for which this alignment setting will apply.
2. From the Main Menu bar, select **Style.**
3. From the Style pull-down, select **Alignment.**
4. In the Style Alignment dialog box, select the point of label alignment in the Align Labels box: **Left, Center,** or **Right.**
5. Optionally, select the check box **Align Over Columns** to position labels relative to the entire range.
6. If you wish to override the range selected in step 1, specify a range name or address in the Range text box.
7. Select **OK.**

• **NOTES** This command has the effect of changing the label prefix character of text data. (See "Entering Data.")

If you are working on a file in GROUP mode, this command affects the same range in all sheets.

Any label that is longer than the column width is aligned left automatically.

• OPTIONS Options in step 4 are Left, Center, or Right relative to the edges of the cell that contains the label. If you select Align Over Columns in step 5, the options refer to the left and right range boundaries, and labels should be only in the far left column. Also, the additional option Even appears, which spreads the label across the range. The Even option ignores labels ending in punctuation marks (. : ! ?).

See Also *Entering Data, Worksheet Global Settings.*

STYLE BORDER

Draws lines around the edges of cells and/or their range, and can add a drop-shadow around the range.

To Border a Range:

1. In the current worksheet window, highlight a range to be bordered.
2. From the Main Menu bar, select **Style.**
3. From the Style pull-down, select **Border.**
4. The Style Border dialog box appears. Select any of the check boxes for border position: **All Edges, Top, Bottom, Left, Right,** and/or **Outline.**
5. For each border position selected in step 4, select a line style in the drop-down box next to it: **Single, Double,** or **Bold.**
6. To add a drop-shadow to the edges of the range, select the **Drop Shadow** check box.
7. If you wish to override the range selected in step 1, specify a range name or address in the Range text box.

8. Select **OK.**

• OPTIONS Options in step 4 are: All Edges (outline each cell), Top (top of each cell), Bottom (bottom of each cell), Left (left of each cell), Right (right of each cell), and/or Outline (around the entire range). Drop Shadow applies only to the range. Any combination of these check boxes can be selected, each with a different line style, if desired.

See Also *File Page Setup, Style Font.*

STYLE COLOR

Permits you to set the text and background colors for a selected range, and optionally specify display of negative values in red. This command applies to monitors and output devices that support color and overrides settings in Window Display Options.

To Specify Colors for a Range:

1. In the current worksheet window, highlight a range to be colored.
2. From the Main Menu bar, select **Style.**
3. From the Style pull-down, select **Color.**
4. The Style Color dialog box appears. Select a color for text in the Cell Contents drop-down box.
5. Select a color for the range background in the Background drop-down box.
6. Optionally, select the check box **Negative Values in Red** to override the selection in step 4 for negative values only.
7. If you wish to override the range selected in step 1, specify a range name or address in the Range text box.
8. Select **OK.**

• NOTE Be sure that the text colors specified in steps 4 and 6 contrast well with the background color you select in step 5. Also, color-blind people might not be able to read red text on a green background.

See Also *File Printer Setup.*

STYLE FONT

Permits you to change the font of displayed items in a selected range, as well as to set attributes Bold, Italics, and Underline. Optionally, you can replace fonts in the current font set.

To Change Font Settings:

1. In the current worksheet window, highlight a range of cells to be formatted.
2. From the Main Menu bar, select **Style.**
3. From the Style pull-down, select **Font.**
4. In the Style Font dialog box, select one of the previously installed fonts and point sizes shown in the Fonts list box.
5. If you wish to override the range selected in step 1, specify a range name or address in the Range text box.
6. Optionally, select any of the attribute check boxes: **Bold, Italics,** or **Underline.**
7. If you select Underline in step 6, choose a line style from the drop-down box: **Single**, **Double**, or **Bold.**

To Replace Fonts in the Current Font Set:

1. From the Main Menu bar, select **Style.**

2. From the Style pull-down, select **Font.**
3. In the Style Font dialog box, select the **Replace** button.
4. The Style Font Replace dialog box appears. From the Current Fonts list box, select a currently installed font that will be replaced.
5. From the Available Fonts list box, select a new font.
6. From the Size list box, select a point size for the new font.
7. Select the **Replace** button.
8. To substitute other fonts in the current font set, repeat steps 4–7.
9. Select **OK.**

• **NOTES** The first font/size shown in the list box in step 4 is the default font. You need not format a range for its contents to be displayed in this font.

If you don't need to change the font, a fast way to set Bold, Italic, or Underline is through the icon palette. Select the range and then simply click on the icon.

When selecting fonts in sizes larger than the default, be sure the column width and row height can accommodate text in the new size. (See "Worksheet Column Width" and "Worksheet Global Settings.")

When working in the Style Font Replace dialog box, to save the current font set as the new default, select **Update.** To return to the program's default set, select **Restore.** To create or get a named font set, select **Save** or **Retrieve** and specify the device, path, and file name.

See Also *Worksheet Column Width, Worksheet Global Settings. Appendix A: SmartIcons. Appendix D: Adobe Type Manager.*

STYLE NAME

Permits you to assign names to style formatting you have established for a worksheet cell. This formatting can then be applied to a selected range in single command simply by selecting the name from the Style pull-down.

To Create Named Styles:

1. In the current worksheet window, highlight a cell to be formatted.
2. Format the cell by making selections from the Style pull-down.
3. From the Main Menu bar, select **Style.**
4. From the Style pull-down, select **Name.**
5. The Style Name dialog box appears. Select the radio button corresponding to the desired style.
6. Enter a style name (1–9 characters) and a description (0–24 characters) in the Name and Description text boxes.
7. If you wish to override the cell address selected in step 1, specify another address in the Range text box.

To Apply a Named Style:

1. In the current worksheet window, highlight a range to be formatted according to the predefined style.
2. From the Main Menu bar, select **Style.**
3. From the Style pull-down, select the name of the style.
4. The Style *Number* dialog box appears. If you wish to override the range selected in step 1, specify a range name or address in the Range text box.
5. Select **OK.**

• **NOTE** Named styles are stored with the worksheet file in which you created them, not as system data files. To use a named style with another file, load both both files into 1-2-3 and use the named style to format a range in the new worksheet.

See Also *Style Font.*

STYLE SHADING

Permits you to add or remove shading, or texture, to or from the background area of a range when it is displayed or printed. This setting can be used with either monochrome or color monitors and output devices. Colored shading is applied according to the settings in Style Color (specific to range) or Window Display Options (global).

To Specify Shading for a Range:

1. In the current worksheet window, highlight a range to be shaded.
2. From the Main Menu bar, select **Style.**
3. From the Style pull-down, select **Shading.**
4. The Style Shading dialog box appears. Select one of the shading options for the range background: **Light, Dark,** or **Solid.**
   or
   To remove a previous shading selection, select **Clear.**
5. If you wish to override the range selected in step 1, specify a range name or address in the Range text box.
6. Select **OK.**

• **NOTES** If you select Dark or Solid shading in step 4, cell contents (text) will be displayed in a light color (in monochrome, white).

Avoid applying shading to large areas if you will be using a dot matrix printer. Avoid shading entirely when using a plotter. Shading works particularly well with laser printers.

See Also *File Page Setup, Style Color, Window Display Options.*

TOOLS ADD-IN

Permits you to load or remove add-ins, or auxiliary programs and files, to or from memory. Add-ins may be provided by third-party vendors and can include application programs, as well as additional @functions or macro commands that extend the capabilities of 1-2-3. Add-ins are stored as files with the extension .ADW and can contain any or all of these elements.

To Load or Remove an Add-In:

1. From the Main Menu bar, select **Tools.**
2. From the Tools pull-down, select **Add-in.**
3. The Tools Add-In dialog box appears. Select the file name of the add-in from the Add-Ins list box.
4. To bring the add-in into memory, select the **Load** button. (If no add-ins are displayed in the list box, you must specify the device, path, and file name in the Tools Add-In Load dialog box, then select **OK.**)
   or
   To remove a previously loaded add-in, select **Remove.**
   or
   To remove all add-ins currently in memory, select **Remove All.**

• **NOTE** If you remove an add-in containing @functions that are referenced in formulas in the current worksheet, the result of the formula will be displayed as **ERR**.

See Also *Part IV: @Functions. Appendix C: Macro Language.*

TOOLS BACKSOLVER

The Backsolver is a special feature of 1-2-3 that calculates the value of the variable in a formula when you specify the desired result of the formula. The calculated variable value must correspond to a cell address in the selected formula.

To Use the Backsolver:

1. Move the cell pointer into the worksheet that contains the formula.
2. From the Main Menu bar, select **Tools.**
3. From the Tools pull-down, select **Backsolver.**
4. The Backsolver dialog box appears. In the Make Cell text box, enter the address of the cell that contains the formula.
5. In the Equal to Value text box, enter the result value.
6. In the By Changing Cell text box, enter the address of the cell to be solved for.
7. Select **Solve.**

• NOTES The Backsolver substitutes values for the variable cell you specify in step 6 until the formula results in the value you specify in step 5. It then displays the solution value in that cell. For the Backsolver to work, the result of the formula must depend on that cell; there cannot be another variable in the formula. The value you enter in step 5 must be numeric or a formula with a numeric result.

You can restore the original value in the test cell (reverse the result of using the Backsolver) if you select **Edit Undo** before executing another command.

See Also *Tools Solver.*

TOOLS MACRO DEBUG

Permits you to inspect the progress of a macro while it is running. Optionally, you can cause the macro to proceed a step at a time while you trace its execution and results. (In 1-2-3, macro instructions are stored in worksheet ranges. See Appendix C: "Macro Language.")

To Debug a Macro:

1. Move the cell pointer to the first cell in a range that holds the macro to be debugged.
2. From the Main Menu bar, select **Tools.**
3. From the Tools pull-down, select **Macro.**
4. From the Macro cascade, select **Debug.**
5. The Tools Macro Debug dialog box appears. Select one or both of the check boxes: **Single Step** and/or **Trace.**
6. Select **OK.**
7. Run the macro. (Select **Tools Macro Run** *or* press **Ctrl-*letter*** for single-letter macro names.)
8. In Step mode, press any key to advance macro execution one step at a time. If Trace is turned on, watch its progress in the Macro Trace window.
9. Edit the macro errors you find in step 8.
10. To end Macro Debug, repeat steps 2–6, but turn off both check boxes before selecting **OK.**

• **NOTES** A macro is a set of commands and/or keystrokes contained in a range. Each command executes one program step, so that running a macro automates a routine, or task. You can record a macro by capturing keystrokes (see "Tools Macro Show Transcript") or by writing a program with a text editor in macro command language.

• **OPTIONS** If Step is turned on in step 5, the macro executes one step or keystroke at a time. Press any key during execution to advance to the next step. If Trace is turned on, the Macro Trace window appears. This window shows the address and contents of the current macro command. If Step is also turned on, a cursor in the command string highlights each keystroke or command as it is executed.

As an alternative to selecting Step in step 5, you can press **Alt-F2** (Step) prior to running a macro. Press it again to cancel Step.

See Also *Tools Macro Run, Tools Macro Show Transcript. Appendix C: Macro Language.*

TOOLS MACRO RUN

Permits you to select and start execution of a macro. (In 1-2-3, macro instructions are stored in worksheet ranges. See Appendix C: "Macro Language.")

To Run a Macro:

1. Move the cell pointer to the first cell in a range that contains the macro to be run.
2. From the Main Menu bar, select **Tools.**
3. From the Tools pull-down, select **Macro.**
4. From the Macro cascade, select **Run.**
5. The Tools Macro Run dialog box appears. The names of all macros in the current worksheet appear in the list box. If you wish to override the range selected in step 1, specify a macro name or address in the Macro Name text box.
6. Select **OK.**

• OPTIONS Enter a single-letter macro name (called a *backslash macro*) as *N*, where *N* is the letter. To run such a macro, simply press **Ctrl** and the letter key at the same time.

See Also *Tools Macro Debug, Tools Macro Show Transcript. Appendix C: Macro Language.*

TOOLS MACRO SHOW TRANSCRIPT

Opens a Transcript window, which displays keystrokes as you record them for purposes of building a macro. You can also edit the contents of the Transcript window, including Edit Copy/Cut to and Edit Paste from, from the Clipboard (scratch-pad memory area in Windows).

To Record a Macro:

1. From the Main Menu bar, select **Tools.**
2. From the Tools pull-down, select **Macro.**
3. From the Macro cascade, select **Show Transcript.**
4. The Transcript window appears, containing all keystrokes you've entered so far in this session of 1-2-3. Click on the window or press **Ctrl-F6** to activate the window.
5. From the Transcript menu bar, select **Edit.**
6. From the Edit pull-down, select **Clear All.** The contents of the Transcript window are cleared, ready for new entries.
7. Move the cell pointer to the worksheet window, or press **Ctrl-F6** to activate it.
8. Perform the program selections and entries you want to capture as a macro. Both keystrokes and mouse actions are permissible.

9. The actions you've performed appear in macro command syntax in the Transcript window. Click on the Transcript window or press **Ctrl-F6** to end the macro entry and activate the Transcript window.
10. If necessary, use commands from the Edit pull-down to edit the macro commands in the Transcript window. (See Appendix C: "Macro Language.")
11. In the Transcript window, highlight all commands in the macro. Then select **Edit Copy** or **Edit Cut** to move the macro from the Transcript window to the Clipboard.
12. Move the cell pointer to the worksheet window, or press **Ctrl-F6** to activate it.
13. Move the cell pointer to the first cell of a range that will hold the new macro.
14. Select **Edit Paste** to copy the macro from the Clipboard into the selected location in the worksheet.
15. Select **Range Name** and name the new macro.
16. If necessary, use **Tools Macro Debug** to find errors in the macro.

• OPTIONS A new menu bar appears at the top of the screen when you activate (click on) the Transcript window. This menu has pull-downs for the following commands:

File Closes the Transcript window or exits the 1-2-3 program.

Edit Copy or Cut the contents of the Transcript window to the Clipboard; Paste from the Clipboard. Clear a command line in the window or Clear All (the entire contents of the window).

Macro Runs the macro in the Transcript window. Pauses recording (select while recording keystrokes), debugs (brings up the Macro Debug dialog box for selecting Step and/or Trace execution). Minimizes on run (shrinks the Transcript window to an icon while the macro is running; conserves memory).

Window Tile or Cascade the Transcript window and active sheet windows. Moves control among open windows.

Help Accesses the 1-2-3 Help system.

See Also *Edit Copy, Edit Cut, Edit Paste, Tools Macro Debug, Tools Macro Run.* Part I: *The Clipboard. Appendix C: Macro Language.*

TOOLS SMARTICONS

Permits you to rearrange the placement of the icon palette on the 1-2-3 screen. Optionally, you can hide the palette or customize the set of icons and their actions. (The icon palette permits you to execute 1-2-3 commands simply by clicking on an icon with the mouse. See Appendix A: "SmartIcons.")

To Rearrange the Palette of SmartIcons:

1. From the Main Menu bar, select **Tools.**
2. From the Tools pull-down, select **SmartIcons.**
3. The Tools SmartIcons dialog box appears. Select a position on the screen for the palette: **Left, Right, Top, Bottom,** or **Floating.**
   or
   To hide the palette, select the Hide Palette check box.
4. Optionally, to customize the icon set, select the **Customize** button. (See "Options," below.)
5. Select **OK.**

• NOTES Settings here also apply to the Graph Tools icon palette. Do not confuse SmartIcons with the Palette in Window Display Options, which controls colors.

• OPTIONS If you specify Floating in step 3, the icon palette appears in a box that you can drag around the screen, and whose dimensions (number of rows and columns of icons) can be easily controlled.

If you select Customize in step 4, the Tools SmartIcons Customize dialog box appears. When you click on any of the icons shown here, the corresponding action appears in the Description text box. You can select standard or custom icons from the list boxes and add them to the Current Palette list box. You can also remove an icon by clicking on its picture in the current palette and selecting the **Remove** button.

Also in this text box, you can assign a macro that you create to an icon. Select an unassigned icon, then select the **Assign Macro** button. The Tools SmartIcons Customize Assign Macro dialog box appears. In the Macro text box, define the macro, or specify in the Range text box the location of an existing macro and select the **Get Macro** button.

See Also Part III: *Tools SmartIcons. Appendix A: SmartIcons.*

TOOLS SOLVER

The Solver is a special feature of 1-2-3 that can solve for all variables in a complex worksheet model. Optionally, the Solver can optimize one of the variables. The Solver presents a range of possible answers, or combinations of variable values.

To Use the Solver:

1. Set up a worksheet model designed for use with the Solver. (See "Notes," below, for requirements.)
2. From the Main Menu bar, select **Tools.**
3. From the Tools pull-down, select **Solver.**
4. The Solver Definition dialog box appears. In the Adjustable Cells text box, enter cell addresses containing problem variables. Insert semicolons (;) as argument separators between multiple addresses.
5. In the Constraint Cells text box, enter the range names or addresses that contain logical formulas for the answer.

6. Optionally, enter the range name or address of a cell to optimize in the Optimal Cell text box. Select one of the radio buttons, **Max** or **Min**, to maximize or minimize this cell's value in the solution.
7. To specify the number of answers the Solver will find, select the **Options** button. The Solver Options dialog box appears. In the Number of Answers text box, enter a number and then select **OK.**
8. Select **Solve.**
9. While the Solver is working, the Solver Progress dialog box appears with status information, including percent complete. To stop execution, select **Cancel** or press **Ctrl-Break.**
10. The Solver displays results in the Solver Answer dialog box. If no answers are found, you are returned to step 4.

• NOTES The three elements required of a model to be used with the Solver are shown in the Solver Definition dialog box. Consider the elements as a set of problems in algebra. The Adjustable Cells are a set of variables. The Constraint Cells are a set of equations (logical formulas) containing the variables. The Optimal Cell, if you decide to use it, can be regarded as the ideal result, such as maximum return on investment or minimum cost.

A comprehensive treatment of the Solver's capabilities is beyond the scope of this book. For more information on building models for this purpose, see the *Solver Guide* supplied with the 1-2-3 package.

• OPTIONS If you specify an Optimal Cell in step 6, its contents must be variable, or it must contain a formula that refers to at least one variable cell. Selecting this option may reduce the number of answers that are required (or possible), both optimizing the solution and speeding execution. The number of answers (1–999) you specify in step 7 is approximate.

See Also *Tools Backsolver.*

TOOLS USER SETUP

Permits you to set various 1-2-3 program parameters, including default worksheet directory, user options, clock display, international formats, and recalculation options.

To Set User Options:

1. From the Main Menu bar, select **Tools.**
2. From the Tools pull-down, select **User Setup.**
3. The Tools User Setup dialog box appears. Select any of the check boxes to set user options: **Beep on Error, Enable Edit Undo**, and **Run Autoexecute Macros.**
4. Select one of the formats for clock display: **Standard**, **International**, or **None.**
5. To change the default worksheet directory, enter a device and path in the Worksheet Directory text box.
6. To set international display formats, select the **International** button. The Tools User Setup International dialog box appears. Make settings and then select **OK.** (See "Options," below.)
7. To include the settings in steps 3–6 in program defaults for future sessions, select **Update.**
8. To set recalculation options, select the **Recalculation** button. The Tools User Setup Recalculation dialog box appears. Make settings and then select **OK.** (See "Options," below.)
9. Select **OK.**

• OPTIONS

User Setup These options can be set in steps 3–5.

Beep on error Sounds the computer bell on program errors and on the macro command {beep}.

Enable Edit Undo Turns on the ability to reverse the previous program selection.

Run autoexecute macros When a file containing a macro is opened, executes the macro automatically.

Clock display Select among: **Standard** (day-month-year and AM/PM), **International** (Long International date *11/06/99* and Short International time *23:59*), and **None** (no display on program status line).

International The following options can be set in the Tools User Setup International dialog box in step 6.

Style For punctuation and argument separators, choose among eight numbered styles in the drop-down box. For display of negative values, choose between **Parentheses** and **Sign** (–) in the drop-down box.

Currency Enter any currency symbol in the text box. Specify the position of the currency symbol as **Prefix** (leading) or **Suffix** (trailing) in the drop-down box.

Format Select date and time display formats from the numbered choices in the drop-down boxes. These settings apply only to Long and Short International options.

File translation Specify whether Release 2 worksheets will be translated according to the Lotus International Character Set (LICS) or ASCII in the 1-2-3 Rel 2 drop-down box. In the other drop-down box, specify whether an imported or created text file will be translated in International format or according to the current system country setting.

Recalculation The following options can be set in the Tools User Setup Recalculation dialog box in step 8:

Order of recalculation Select one: **Natural** (recalculate source formulas first), **Columnwise** (left to right by column, from top to bottom sheet), or **Rowwise** (top to bottom by row, from top to bottom sheet).

Recalculation Select one: **Automatic** (on each new entry), or **Manual** (when you press F9 (Calc)).

Iterations Enter a number (1–50) for the number of columnwise or rowwise passes, or when you have selected Natural for a circular reference (recursion).

See Also *Worksheet Global Settings.* Part I: *Install 1-2-3.*

WINDOW CASCADE/TILE

Control the display of document windows in 1-2-3 when multiple sheets/files are open. Document windows include worksheets, graphs, and transcripts. Select **Cascade** to show windows in stair-step arrangement with only the title bars of obscured windows showing (see Figure II.9). Or, select **Tile** to show windows side-by-side (see Figure II.10).

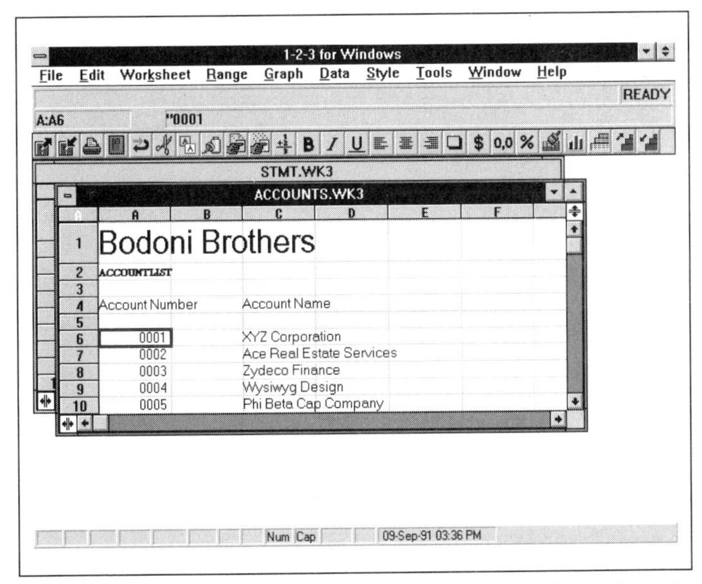

Figure II.9: Document windows arranged with Windows Cascade

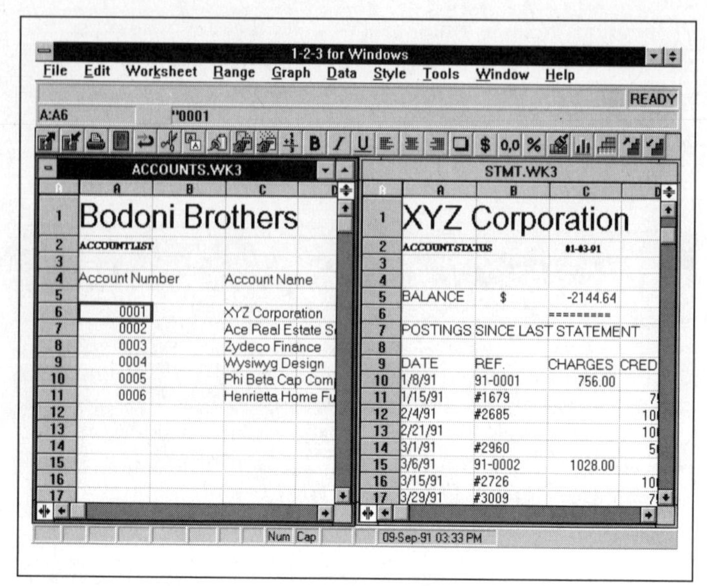

Figure II.10: Document windows arranged with Windows Tile

To Control Document Window Display:

1. From the Main Menu bar, select **Window.**
2. From the Window pull-down select either **Cascade** or **Tile.**

WINDOW DISPLAY OPTIONS

Permits you to set various options regarding the display of worksheets. Settings can be made to apply only to the current session or to update default settings that will control future sessions.

To Set Window Display Options:

1. From the Main Menu bar, select **Window.**
2. From the Window pull-down, select **Display Options.**
3. The Window Display Options dialog box appears. Make selections for Color, Options, Zoom, and Frame.
4. To pick a different set of colors, select **Palette,** pick a current palette color, then make a new selection from in the Colors box. Select **OK.**
5. To make settings apply to future sessions, select the **Update** button. To return to prior default values, select **Restore.**
6. Select **OK.**

• OPTIONS The following options can be set in the Window Display Options dialog box in step 3.

Colors Select among eight colors (or **Clear**) from drop-down boxes for each category: Worksheet Frame, Cell Background, Cell Contents, Negative Values, Drop Shadows, Grid Lines, Range Borders, Selected Ranges, and Unprotected Cells. (To change the set of colors available, select the **Palette** button and do step 4.)

Options Select any or all of the following check boxes: **Page Breaks** (on = display the breaks), **Draft** (on = low resolution display; off = graphic display), **B&W** (monochrome output), and **Grid Lines** (on = display the lines).

Zoom Enter a value from 25–400 for percent of magnification of cells in the worksheet document window.

Frame Select the units of measure for rulers, if any, around the edge of worksheet document windows: **Standard** (gray frame, no rulers), **Characters** (10-point), **Inches**, **Metric** (centimeters), **Points/Picas**, or **None** (hide the frame).

WINDOW *FILENAME*

Items correspond to worksheet files that are currently open. A check mark (✓) in the pull-down indicates the file that is active. Use this command to move among document windows.

To Change the Active Document Window:

1. From the Main Menu bar, select **Window.**
   or
   Click on the title bar of the window you want to activate. Skip step 2.
2. From the Window pull-down, select the ***Filename*** of the window to activate.

WINDOW SPLIT

Permits you to subdivide a worksheet so that you can view two different portions of it in the same document window. Optionally, you can cause these two *panes* to be synchronized, or scroll together. Also, contiguous worksheets can be shown in perspective.

To Split a Window:

1. Move the cell pointer to the location in the current document window at which the window will be split.
2. From the Main Menu bar, select **Window.**
   or
   With the mouse, drag the symbol with the double-arrowhead to mark the boundary of the panes. Drag the symbol in the top right corner downward for a vertical split, or drag the symbol in the bottom right corner to the right for a horizontal split (see Figure II.11). Skip steps 3–6.

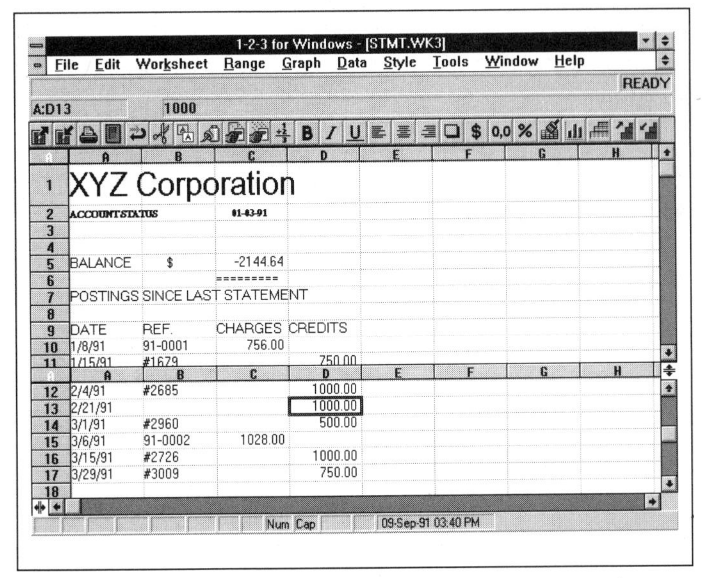

Figure II.11: A worksheet window split into two panes with Windows Split Horizontal

3. From the Window pull-down, select **Split.**
4. The Window Split dialog box appears. Select the split type: **Horizontal, Vertical, Perspective,** or **Clear.**
5. To make the split views scroll together, turn the Synchronize toggle on.
6. Select **OK.**

• NOTES When you use the mouse method in step 1, the panes are synchronized by default. Split will not work from the command menu unless you first specify a column or row location in step 1. The Perspective option will not work properly unless the current file contains multiple sheets.

• OPTIONS Options in step 4 are: Horizontal (split at the current row), Vertical (split at the current column), Perspective (three contiguous sheets), or Clear (undo a previous split; fill the window with one view).

See Also *Window Cascade/Tile.*

WORKSHEET COLUMN WIDTH

Sets the width of a specified column or columns in a worksheet (see Figure II.12). Optionally, you can reset the width to a global default value.

To Set Column Width:

1. In the current worksheet window, highlight a range containing the columns to be adjusted.

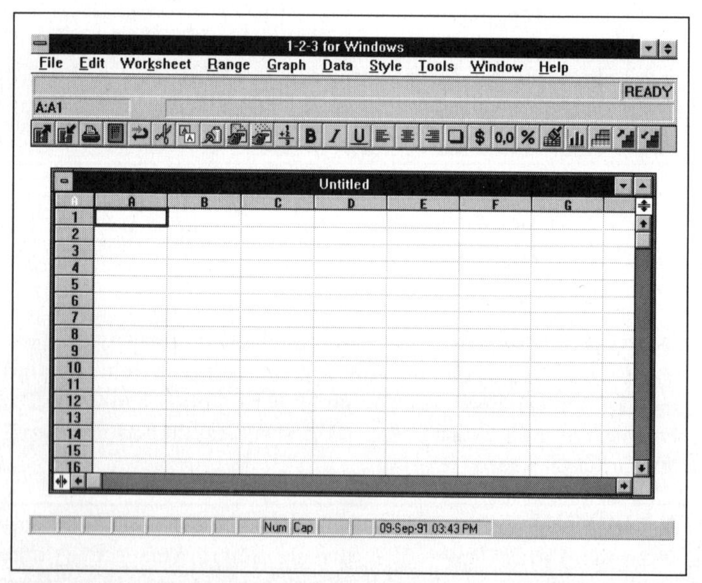

Figure II.12: The default worksheet screen

or

With the mouse, move the cell pointer to the column-letter heading, drag the right column border to the desired width, and skip steps 2–6. (The program must be in READY mode.)

2. From the Main Menu bar, select **Worksheet.**
3. From the Worksheet pull-down, select **Column Width.**
4. In the Worksheet Column Width dialog box, enter the new width in characters (1–240) in the Set Width To text box.

   or

   Select **Reset to Global** to change the column width back to the global setting.
5. If you wish to override the range selected in step 1, specify a range name or address in the Range text box.
6. Select **OK.**

• NOTES When the worksheet file is in GROUP mode, this command affects all sheets in the file.

The number of characters that can be displayed in a column depends on both the width setting in step 4 and the current font size. For example, you can display more characters in a given width by reducing the font size. The default is a 9-character column width in Swiss 12 point.

If the adjacent cell to the right contains data, the program truncates the display of any label that does not fit in the specified column width. Otherwise, if the adjacent cells are blank, the label is run across them.

For correct display of numeric values, the column must be one character wider than the value format. If a value as formatted will not fit in the specified width, the program displays asterisks (***) in place of the value. To adjust the display format instead of column width, use **Range Format.**

• OPTIONS Options in step 4 are the following:

Set Width To Enter a number from 1–240 for the column width.

Reset to Global Returns the column width to the setting made with Worksheet Global Settings Column Width, which affects all columns not explicitly reset.

See Also *Range Format, Style Font, Worksheet Global Settings.*

WORKSHEET DELETE

Deletes cells and their data in the current worksheet. Optionally, you can delete columns or rows in a specified range, or the entire contents of one or more sheets. Deleted cells are removed from the sheet. Column/row numbers, as well as addresses in range names and formulas, are adjusted accordingly.

To Delete Data:

1. In the current worksheet window, highlight a range of data to be deleted.
2. From the Main Menu bar, select **Worksheet.**
3. From the Worksheet pull-down, select **Delete.**
4. In the Worksheet Delete dialog box, select **Column, Row,** or **Sheet.**
5. If you wish to override the range selected in step 1, specify a range name or address in the Range text box.
6. Select **OK.**

• **NOTES** To cancel the results of this command, use **Edit Undo** before you do anything else.

The range specified in steps 1 or 5 must contain at least one cell from each of the columns, rows, or sheets that will be deleted.

If a formula contains a reference to a deleted cell or range, its result is displayed as **ERR**. If a formula refers to a named range that no longer exists, the range is regarded as undefined.

When the current file is in GROUP mode, this command makes the deletion at the same location in each sheet in the file. (For more information on GROUP mode, see "Worksheet Global Settings.")

To simply remove an entire file from memory, use **File Close.** (You will be asked whether you wish to save it first.)

• **OPTIONS** In step 4, you have the following options:

Column Within the specified range, deletes all columns.

Rows Within the specified range, deletes all rows.

Sheet Deletes the entire worksheet currently containing the cell pointer.

See Also *Edit Clear, File Close, Range Addressing, Worksheet Global Settings.*

WORKSHEET GLOBAL SETTINGS

Sets various parameters that affect the display of the current worksheet and its value formats. These settings are global, or affect the entire sheet, and may be overridden by explicit commands like Worksheet Column Width, Style Alignment, and so on. Settings apply to all sheets in the current file if GROUP mode is turned on in this command's options.

To Make Global Worksheet Settings:

1. Move the cell pointer into the worksheet document window to be affected.
2. From the Main Menu bar, select **Worksheet.**
3. From the Worksheet pull-down, select **Global Settings.**

4. In the Worksheet Global Settings dialog box, you can reset the following options: Zero Display, Align Labels, Group Mode, Protection, and Column Width.
5. Also in the dialog box, select **Format** to change the display formats of numbers, labels, dates, times, and so on.
6. In the Worksheet Global Settings Format dialog box, make selections for the options Format, Decimal Places, and Parentheses. Then select **OK.**
7. In the Worksheet Global Settings dialog box, Select **OK.**

• NOTE If you specify anything other than General in Format options, you must also make an entry in the Decimal Places text box.

• OPTIONS Options in the dialog boxes in steps 4 and 6 include the following:

Zero Display If the contents of a cell equal zero, shows the results as zeros, leaves zeros blank, or uses a label (enter a label in the text box).

Align Labels For text labels, or alphanumeric data preceded by a label prefix ('), select **Left, Center**, or **Right** to justify the string in the column.

Group Mode Turns GLOBAL mode on and off. When on, Worksheet Global Settings affect all sheets in the current file.

Protection When this toggle is on, the current worksheet is protected, or has read-only status. You can then make changes only to cells that you explicitly unprotect with the Range Unprotect command.

Column Width Enter a value from 1–240 for the global width of all columns in the worksheet. Individual columns can be adjusted with the Worksheet Column Width command.

Format Options in the dialog box in step 6 include the following:

Format Select among: **Fixed** (truncated to the specified number of decimal places), **Scientific** (power of 10), **Currency** (sign and decimal), **Comma** (thousands separator), **General** (default, no thousands separator), **+/–** (bar graph equivalent), **Percent** (calculated, with % sign), **Text** (formulas as text, numbers as General), **Hidden** (not printed), **Automatic** (program determines best fit), **Label** (label prefix (') added automatically), or numbered date and time formats 1–9.

Parentheses Encloses minus values in parentheses ( ).

Decimal places Enter a value from 1–15 for the number of digits to the right of the decimal point.

See Also *Range Format, Range Unprotect, Worksheet Column Width.*

WORKSHEET HIDE

Prevents display and printing of data in the specified range. Optionally, you can hide columns in a specified range, or the entire contents of one or more sheets. The effect of this command is to make the format of each cell in the specified range Hidden.

To Hide Data:

1. In the current worksheet window, highlight a range of columns to be hidden.
   or
   With the mouse, move the cell pointer to the column-letter heading and then drag the right border of the column or block of columns *leftward* until it touches the left border—in effect, folding it over on itself. Skip steps 2–6.
2. From the Main Menu bar, select **Worksheet.**
3. From the Worksheet pull-down, select **Hide.**
4. In the Worksheet Hide dialog box, select **Column** or **Sheet.**
5. If you wish to override the range selected in step 1, specify a range name or address in the Range text box.
6. Select **OK.**

• NOTES When a column is hidden, it retains its column-letter address. In READY mode, the column will not appear on the worksheet, and its column letter will be missing from the column-letter sequence in the worksheet heading. The column will appear in POINT mode, with an asterisk (*) next to its column letter to indicate that its data are hidden. You can work with the data in hidden cells in POINT mode, but not in READY mode. Formulas in hidden cells continue to operate in all modes.

To cancel the results of executing this command, use **Worksheet Unhide.** To hide data in a range, use **Range Format** instead. To hide all data in a worksheet, you can also use **Worksheet Global Settings Format.**

To hide columns, the range specified in steps 1 or 5 must contain at least one cell from each of the columns that will be hidden, and you must then specify **Column** in step 4.

• OPTIONS In step 4, select **Column** to hide columns in the specified range, or **Sheet** to hide all data in the current worksheet.

See Also *Range Format, Worksheet Global Settings, Worksheet Unhide.*

WORKSHEET INSERT

Permits you to insert columns or rows into the current worksheet, as well as multiple sheets into the current worksheet file.

To Make Insertions:

1. In the current worksheet window, highlight a range at the point of insertion that includes the same number of columns/rows to be inserted.
2. From the Main Menu bar, select **Worksheet.**
3. From the Worksheet pull-down, select **Insert.**

4. In the Worksheet Insert dialog box, select **Column, Row,** or **Sheet.**
5. If you selected Sheet in step 4, specify where to insert the new sheets by selecting **Before** or **After** (relative to the current sheet) and enter the number of sheets in the Quantity text box.
6. If you wish to override the range selected in step 1, specify a range name or address in the Range text box.
7. Select **OK.**

• NOTES The range selected in step 1 or 6 must span the number of columns or rows to be inserted. The point of insertion is either to the left (for Column) or above (for Row) the specified range.

The program adjusts formulas and references unless addresses are specified as absolute with the $ syntax. (See "Range Addressing.")

To open a new worksheet file, use **File New.**

When the current file is in GROUP mode, the Worksheet Insert command for Column or Row makes an insertion at the same location in each sheet in the file.

• OPTIONS You can select the following options in steps 4 and 5:

Column Blank columns appear to the left of the specified range. The number of columns inserted is the same as the number of columns in the specified range. Inserting the columns on the left moves the existing data to the right. Column letters are adjusted.

Row Blank rows appear above the specified range. The number of rows inserted is the same as the number of rows in the specified range. Inserting the rows above the range moves the existing data downward. Row numbers are adjusted.

Sheet This option inserts new sheets into the current worksheet file according to the selections in step 5:

Before or **After** Indicate the point of insertion relative to the current worksheet.

Quantity Enter the number of new sheets to be inserted.

See Also *File New.*

WORKSHEET PAGE BREAK

Controls where new pages will begin when a worksheet file is printed. If GROUP mode is on, this command will apply to all worksheets in the file.

To Specify Page Breaks:

1. Move the cell pointer to the leftmost column and top row of the new page.
2. From the Main Menu bar, select **Worksheet.**
3. From the Worksheet pull-down, select **Page Break.**
4. In the Worksheet Page Break dialog box, select **Horizontal, Vertical, Both,** or **Clear.**
5. Select **OK.**

• NOTES Page-length settings in File Print and File Page Setup are overridden by this command.

A dashed line in the document window indicates a page break if page-break display is set in Window Display Options.

• OPTIONS Select one of the following options in step 4:

Horizontal Makes the row in which the cell pointer is located the top of the page.

Vertical Makes the column in which the cell pointer is located the leftmost column of the page.

Both Makes the cell in which the cell pointer is located the top left corner of the page.

Clear Deletes a previously inserted page break at the cell pointer location.

See Also *File Page Setup, File Print, Window Display Options, Worksheet Global Settings.*

WORKSHEET ROW HEIGHT

Sets the height of rows in terms of the point size of the current font. Optionally, you can reset row height to the default.

To Set Row Height:

1. In the current worksheet window, highlight a range of rows to be adjusted.
   or
   With the mouse, move the cell pointer to the row-number area and then drag the bottom border of a row to adjust the row height. Skip steps 2–6. (The program must be in READY mode.)
2. From the Main Menu bar, select **Worksheet.**
3. From the Worksheet pull-down, select **Row Height.**
4. In the Worksheet Row Height dialog box, select **Set Height To** and enter the height in points (1–255) in the text box.
   or
   Select **Reset Height** to return to the default.
5. If you wish to override the range selected in step 1, specify a range name or address in the Range text box.
6. Select **OK.**

• NOTES Regardless of the settings you make here, the program will adjust row height to fit the largest font specified in that row. To reduce the row height, it may also be necessary to reset font size with Style Font.

See Also *Style Font.*

WORKSHEET TITLES

Permits you to specify columns and rows to hold labels for titles in the current worksheet. Titles then remain when you scroll the worksheet and are printed on each output page. If GROUP mode is on, this command will apply to all worksheets in the file.

To Locate Worksheet Titles:

1. Move the cell pointer to the location below and to the right of the area that will contain the titles.
2. From the Main Menu bar, select **Worksheet.**
3. From the Worksheet pull-down, select **Titles.**
4. In the Worksheet Titles dialog box, select **Horizontal, Vertical, Both,** or **Clear.**
5. Select **OK.**

• NOTES Once you have specified a title area, you cannot move the cell pointer there when the program is in READY mode. Press **F5** (Go to) and enter a cell address. You can then edit the titles, if you wish.

• OPTIONS In step 4, select one of the following options:

Horizontal Makes the row in which the cell pointer is located the lower boundary of the title area.

Vertical Makes the column in which the cell pointer is located the rightmost boundary of the title area.

Both Marks the cell in which the cell pointer is located as the lower right corner of the title area.

Clear Releases previously specified title areas.

See Also *Worksheet Global Settings.*

WORKSHEET UNHIDE

Reverses the result of a previous Worksheet Hide command.

To Unhide a Worksheet:

1. In the current worksheet window, highlight a range of columns to be revealed.
   or
   With the mouse, move the cell pointer to the column-letter heading. Drag the right border of the left-adjacent column or block of columns *rightward* until the hidden data are revealed. Skip steps 2–6.
2. From the Main Menu bar, select **Worksheet.**
3. From the Worksheet pull-down, select **Unhide.**
4. In the Worksheet Unhide dialog box, select **Column** or **Sheet.**
5. If you wish to override the range selected in step 1, specify a range name or address in the Range text box.
6. Select **OK.**

• NOTES To use this command, you must have previously hidden the data with Worksheet Hide. To "unhide" data in a range, reset Range Format instead. To unhide all data in a worksheet, you can reset Worksheet Global Settings Format.

To unhide columns, the range specified in steps 1 or 5 must contain at least one cell from each of the columns that will be revealed, and you must then specify **Column** in step 4.

• OPTIONS In step 4, select **Column** to reveal selected columns in the specified range, or **Sheet** to reveal all hidden data in the current worksheet.

See Also *Range Format, Worksheet Global Settings, Worksheet Hide.*

Part Three

The Graph Window Menu

This portion of the book covers pull-down commands, or submenu items, within the Graph window menu. The Graph menu bar appears when you select Graph New (to create a new chart), Graph View (to look at an existing chart), or Graph Add to Sheet (to merge an existing graph) from the 1-2-3 Main Menu. The pull-downs of the Graph menu bar, from left to right across the screen, are: File, Edit, Chart, Draw, Layout, Rearrange, Style, Tools, Window, and Help. (Help commands are discussed in Part I, "Help.")

In 1-2-3, the name of a command usually includes all the menu and submenu items that you must select to execute the command. In this part of the book, entry headings for the Graph Window menu are assumed to start with Graph New/View/Add, so this part of the command is omitted. For example, you will find a description of the command Graph Chart Data Labels Group Range under the entry "Chart Data Labels." The Group Range settings are described under the subheading "Options." The Graph pull-down entries from the Main Menu are also covered in this part.

CHART AXIS

Sets parameters for the X, Y, and optional second Y (2nd Y) axes of graphs (Figures III.1 and III.2).

To Define Chart Axes:

1. From the Main Menu bar, select **Graph.**
2. From the Graph pull-down, select **New** (for a new chart) or **View** (for an existing chart).
3. In the dialog box that appears, specify a graph name and select **OK.**
4. The Graph menu bar appears. Select **Chart.**

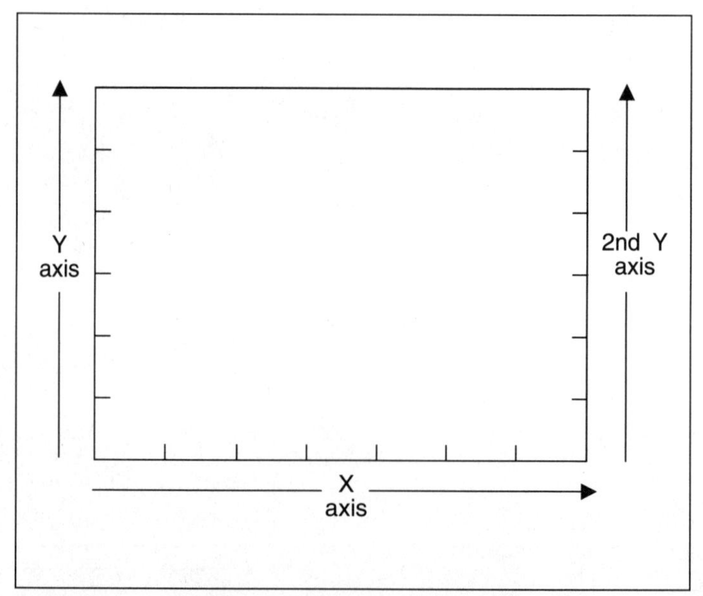

Figure III.1: A chart with X, Y, and 2nd Y axes, in vertical orientation

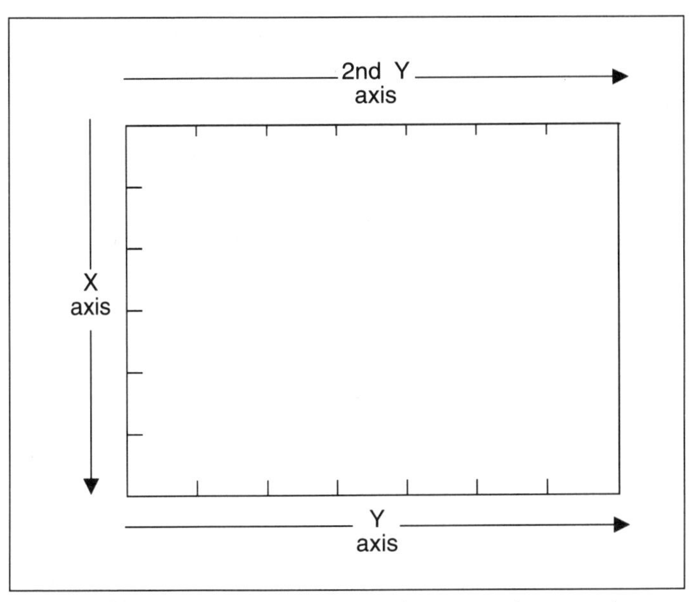

Figure III.2: A chart with X, Y, and 2nd Y axes, in horizontal orientation

5. From the Chart pull-down, select **Axis.**
6. From the Axis cascade, select **X, Y,** or **2nd Y.**
7. In the Chart Axis X/Y/2ndY dialog box, set options for Scale Axis, Axis Units, and Type of Scale. (See "Options," below.)
8. In the dialog box, select **Format,** then set Format and Decimal Places in the Chart Axis X/Y/2ndY Format dialog box. Select **OK.**
9. Also in the dialog box, select **Options.** The Chart Axis X/Y/2ndY Options dialog box appears. Enter an axis title in the Axis Title text box and make selections in the Name of Units and Display Label Every *N* Ticks text boxes. Then select **OK.**
10. When you have finished making settings in the Chart Axis X/Y/2ndY dialog box, select **OK.**

• NOTES Use dual Y axes when plotting two or more data ranges that have different units or orders of magnitude. (The second Y axis on charts in vertical orientation runs along the right vertical edge of the graph area.) The objective of dual Y plotting usually is to look for corresponding fluctuations and trends. For clarity, use a color-coding scheme to associate a data range with its Y axis.

If you define scale boundaries with the Manual option, do not specify an upper limit that is less than the lower limit. If you do, the program will simply display a blank graph window.

If you make both X and Y axes logarithmic (log-log plotting), don't specify a linear (Standard) second Y axis. Semi-log and log plots are typically used in scientific and engineering applications to show data items of widely different magnitudes on the same graph. However, avoid these formats if your audience is unfamiliar with logarithmic plotting.

When specifying axis title and name of units in step 9, precede a cell address or range names with a backslash (\) to pick up a label already in the worksheet. If you enter a range name here, the program will use the label in the first cell in the range.

• OPTIONS The following options can be set in the dialog boxes in steps 7–10:

Scale Axis If you select Automatic (the default), the program calculates a scale that fits the data range. If you select Manual, you must enter lower and upper data range boundaries in the text boxes for Show Values Between.

Axis Units If you select Automatic (the default), the program calculates the order of magnitude for scale values, based on the data ranges. If you select Manual, you must enter an exponent (power of 10) in the corresponding text box ($-95 <= E <= 95$). For example, for a scale 0–20,000, you would enter an exponent of 4 to indicate 10^4.

Type of Scale Specify **Standard** (linear) or **Logarithmic.** If you make only one of the scales (X or Y) logarithmic, a semi-log plot will be generated. Specify both as logarithmic for log-log plotting. For Y and second Y axes, you can specify **Percentage** instead, which calculates and displays the percentage of each data value to the total of values in a range.

Format Selecting the Format button in step 8 lets you set the following options:

Format Select among **Fixed** (truncated to the specified number of decimal places), **Scientific** (power of 10), **Currency** (sign and decimal), **Comma** (thousands separator), **General** (default, no thousands separator), **+/–** (bar graph equivalent), **Percent** (calculated, with % sign), **Text** (formulas as text, numbers as General), **Hidden** (not printed), and **Numbered date and time formats 1–9.**

Decimal places Enter a value from 1–15 for the number of digits to the right of the decimal point for numeric values.

Options Selecting the Options button in step 9 lets you set the following options:

Axis title Enter a text string up to 256 characters long, or enter a backslash (\) and a cell address or range that contains a label.

Name of units Enter a text string as a label for scale units (for example, MILLIONS) or enter a backslash (\) and a cell address or range that contains a label.

Display label every *N* ticks Enter a whole number for the interval at which labels will be placed on the scale. The label will be the axis value at that point. For example, enter 5 to display a label at every fifth tick.

See Also *Chart Data Labels, Chart Legend.* Part II: *Range Addressing, Range Format, Range Name Create, Tools User Setup.*

CHART BORDERS/GRIDS

Lets you set options for borders and grid lines in graph displays and outputs.

To Set Borders and/or Grids:

1. From the Main Menu bar, select **Graph.**
2. From the Graph pull-down, select **New** (for a new chart) or **View** (for an existing chart).
3. In the dialog box that appears, specify a graph name and select **OK.**
4. The Graph menu bar appears. Select **Chart.**
5. From the Chart pull-down, select **Borders/Grids.**
6. In the Chart Borders/Grids dialog box, select any of the check boxes for borders and grid lines. (See "Options," below.)
7. Select **OK.**

• **OPTIONS** Settings in the dialog box in step 6 include the following:

Borders Sets the edge(s) on which borders will be drawn around graphed data. Select check boxes for any combination of these options: **Left, Right, Top,** and **Bottom.**

Grid lines Generates lines at scale divisions perpendicular to the axis selected: **X, Y,** and/or **2nd Y.** X grid lines are vertical and Y grids are horizontal. Select any combination (but usually not *both* Y and 2nd Y.)

See Also *Chart Axis.*

CHART CLEAR

Erases data ranges and/or settings in the current chart.

To Clear Chart Data or Settings:

1. From the Main Menu bar, select **Graph.**

2. From the Graph pull-down, select **New** (for a new chart) or **View** (for an existing chart).
3. In the dialog box that appears, specify a graph name and select **OK.**
4. The Graph menu bar appears. Select **Chart.**
5. From the Chart pull-down, select **Clear.**
6. In the Chart Clear dialog box, select the check boxes corresponding to the items to be cleared. (See "Options," below.)
7. Select **OK.**

• **OPTIONS** Options in the dialog box in step 6 include the following:

Data ranges Marks data ranges selectively, by letter, for clearing. Includes data values and data labels, but omits chart settings. Select **X** and/or any of the **Y ranges A–F,** or **All.** This option also deletes the range definition from the graph.

Entire chart Simply clears all data values and data labels from the current chart.

Chart settings Clears chart settings only, including data labels, but retains data values unless the above options are set.

See Also *Graph Name.* Part II: *Edit Clear Special.*

CHART DATA LABELS

Permits you to specify labels for data points or bars, and to select the positions of those labels relative to the points. Labels are picked up from cells in the worksheet. Ranges that contain labels can be specified selectively for graph data ranges A–F or as a group.

To Pick Up Data Labels from a Worksheet:

1. From the Main Menu bar, select **Graph.**
2. From the Graph pull-down, select **New** (for a new chart) or **View** (for an existing chart).
3. In the dialog box that appears, specify a graph name and select **OK.**
4. The Graph menu bar appears. Select **Chart.**
5. From the Chart pull-down, select **Data Labels.**
6. In the Chart Data Labels dialog box, enter addresses or names of ranges containing labels in the text boxes for graph data ranges A–F.
   or
   To specify labels for graph ranges as a group, select the **Group Range** button, choose options in the Chart Data Labels Group Range dialog box, and select **OK.** (See "Options," below.)
7. In the drop-down boxes to the right of each graph data range text box, select the position relative to the data point or bar at which the label will be displayed: **Above, Center** (the default), **Below, Left**, or **Right.**
8. Select **OK.**

• NOTES A worksheet label range should contain the same number of cells as there are data values in the graph data range. That is, there should be one label for each data value.

If you choose Center, Left, or Right for label position on a bar graph, the labels are actually placed above the bars. In a stacked bar chart, labels are placed inside the bar segments, regardless of the position selected.

To label data points selectively, leave the corresponding positions in the label range blank.

This command applies to line, bar, and area charts. Use **Chart Ranges** to specify label positions on pie charts.

• OPTIONS Settings in the dialog boxes in steps 6 and 7 include the following:

For Selected Graph Ranges If you don't use the Group Range button, specify label ranges in the worksheet for each graph data range A–F (Figures III.3 and III.4).

Data label ranges Enter the addresses or names of ranges that contain labels for graph data ranges A–F. Labels can be text labels, data values, or the current results of a formula at that address.

Label position Sets the position of labels relative to data points in line graphs, and to bars or areas, as follows: Above, Center (the default), Below, Left, or Right.

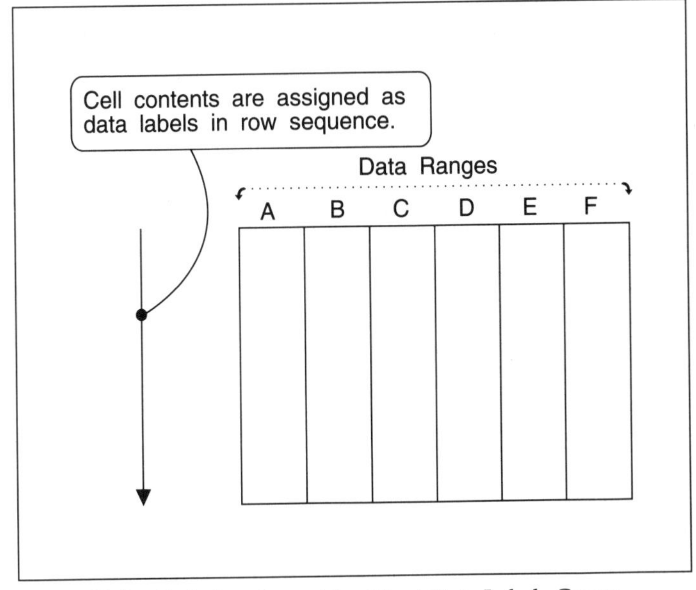

Figure III.3: Worksheet layout for Chart Data Labels Group Range, columnwise

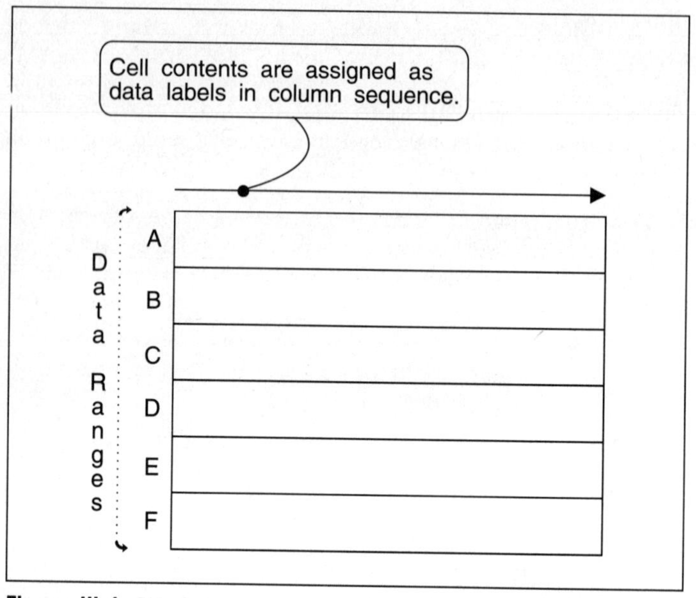

Figure III.4: Worksheet layout for Chart Data Labels Group Range, rowwise

Group Range If you select the Group Range button in step 6, specify how labels will be picked up from a range in the worksheet, by using the following:

Divide into data label ranges Subdivides a worksheet range that contains labels and assigns them to graph data ranges, either by columns (Columnwise) or by rows (Rowwise). For example, if you select Columnwise, the first column in the worksheet is assigned to graph data range A, the second to B, the third to C, and so on.

Range Specifies the address or name of a range that contains all labels for graph data ranges.

Label position Sets the position of labels as described for selected graph ranges, except the default is Above.

See Also *Chart Clear, Chart Ranges.*

CHART HEADINGS

Permits you to enter a title, subtitle, and footnotes to a chart.

To Add Headings to a Chart

1. From the Main Menu bar, select **Graph.**
2. From the Graph pull-down, select **New** (for a new chart) or **View** (for an existing chart).
3. In the dialog box that appears, specify a graph name and select **OK.**
4. The Graph menu bar appears. Select **Chart.**
5. From the Chart pull-down, select **Headings.**
6. In the Chart Headings dialog box, enter text strings or range references in the corresponding text boxes: Title, Subtitle, Note, and 2nd Note.
7. Select **OK.**

• **NOTE** In step 6, precede cell addresses or range names with a backslash (\). Specifying a range reference here will pick up the label at that address. If you specify a range rather than a single cell, the program will use the label in the first cell of the range. Labels can be text labels, data values, or the current value of a formula at that address.

Titles and subtitles are centered above the graph area, and footnotes are positioned bottom left.

Strings of 250 or more characters can be entered, but the display of headings will be controlled by the font size specified in Chart Options Fonts. If a text line overflows the screen, it will be truncated on the right.

See Also *Chart Options.*

CHART LEGEND

Generates a legend with labeled color/symbol/hatch codes for each graph data range. Legend text can be entered selectively for graph data ranges A–F or as a group by specifying a worksheet range that contains labels. (See Figure III.5.)

To Create a Chart Legend:

1. From the Main Menu bar, select **Graph.**
2. From the Graph pull-down, select **New** (for a new chart) or **View** (for an existing chart).
3. In the dialog box that appears, specify a graph name and select **OK.**

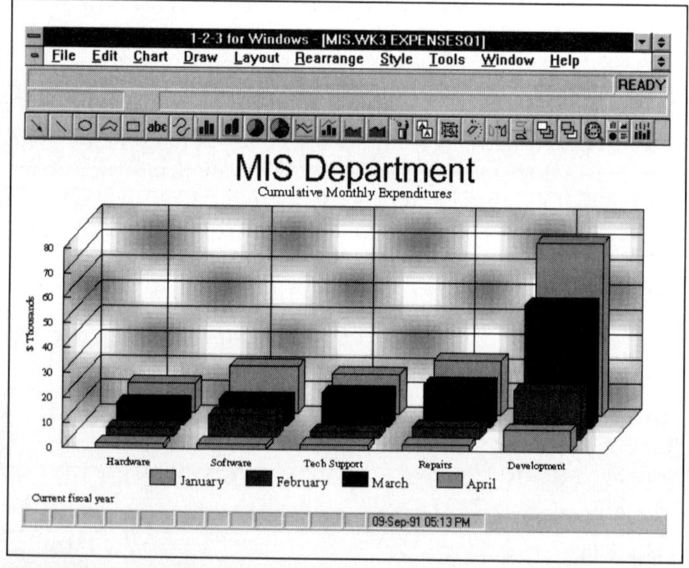

Figure III.5: A sample 3D Bar chart generated by 1-2-3, inclucing a legend

4. The Graph menu bar appears. Select **Chart.**
5. From the Chart pull-down, select **Legend.**
6. In the Chart Legend dialog box, enter text strings or range references for labels in the text boxes for graph data ranges A–F.
   or
   To specify labels for graph ranges as a group, select the **Group Range** button, and in the Chart Legend Group Range dialog box, enter the range address or name that holds the labels. Select **OK.**
7. Select **OK.**

• NOTES In step 6, precede cell addresses or range names with a backslash (\). Specifying a range reference here will pick up the label at that address. If you specify a range rather than a single cell, the program will use the label in the first cell of the range. Labels can be text labels, data values, or the current value of a formula at that address.

The legend will be displayed below the graph area.

If you select the Group Range button in step 6, legend labels will be picked up from the Range you specify. The contents of each cell in the range is used as a label for the legend. Cells in the range are assigned in order to graph data ranges A–F. Similarly, pie slices 1–6 are labeled in counterclockwise order around the pie, starting with the first slice.

See Also *Chart Axis, Chart Headings.*

CHART OPTIONS

Sets various options for chart appearance, including colors, hatch patterns, fonts, and line styles. Optionally, you can define Advanced Styles that pick up styles from ranges in the worksheet.

To Set Chart Options:

1. From the Main Menu bar, select **Graph.**
2. From the Graph pull-down, select **New** (for a new chart) or **View** (for an existing chart).
3. In the dialog box that appears, specify a graph name and select **OK.**
4. The Graph menu bar appears. Select **Chart.**
5. From the Chart pull-down, select **Options.**
6. From the Options cascade, select the category of options to be set: **Colors, Hatches, Fonts, Lines,** or **Advanced Styles.**
7. A dialog box appears with selections for the options category. For colors, hatches, and fonts, make selections from drop-down boxes.
   or
   For lines, select check boxes for the desired attributes.
   or
   For Advanced Styles, enter worksheet range references containing color or hatch styles to be assigned to graph data ranges A–F.
8. Select **OK.**

• NOTES On monochrome outputs generated by laser and dot-matrix printers and by plotters, use hatches instead of colors. Use colors *and* hatches on multicolor printers and plotters to avoid filling large areas with solid color.

• OPTIONS The following options can be set in step 7:

Colors In the Chart Options Colors dialog box, drop-down boxes with color selections appear for Chart Title; Subtitle, Axis Titles, and Legend; Labels, Notes, and Name of Units; and Data Range Colors A–F. Selecting the patch labeled **H** hides that entity. (To set colors in 1-2-3, use **Window Display Options Palette.**)

Hatches In the Chart Options Hatches dialog box, drop-down boxes with hatch patterns appear for graph data ranges A–F. Hatches can be defined for bars, areas, and pie slices.

Fonts In the Chart Options Fonts dialog box, drop-down boxes with font names and sizes appear for Chart Title; Subtitle, Axis Titles, and Legend; and Labels, Notes, and Name of Units.

Lines In the Chart Options Lines dialog box, check boxes for each line style appear for graph data ranges A–F. For each data range, select any combination of styles: **Connectors** (connect the data points), **Symbols** (place a symbol at each data point), and/or **Area Fill** (fill the area under the line with color and/or hatch). If you select Area Fill, specify the color and pattern of the fill with **Chart Options Colors** and **Chart Options Hatches.**

Advanced Styles In the Chart Options Advanced Styles dialog box, enter range references (addresses or names preceded by a backslash (\)) that contain color and/or hatch styles to be applied to each graph data range. The first column of text boxes is for colors and the second column is for hatches.

See Also *Chart Type.* Part II: *Window Display Options.*

CHART RANGES

Lets you assign worksheet ranges to the X axis and graph data ranges A–F. Optionally, you can specify that any of the graph data ranges will be plotted against a second Y (2nd Y) axis. Graph data ranges can also be defined as a group, based on a single, specially designed range in the worksheet.

To Assign Data Ranges for Charting:

1. From the Main Menu bar, select **Graph.**
2. From the Graph pull-down, select **New** (for a new chart) or **View** (for an existing chart).
3. In the dialog box that appears, specify a graph name and select **OK.**

4. The Graph menu bar appears. Select **Chart.**
5. From the Chart pull-down, select **Ranges.**
6. In the Chart Ranges dialog box, enter the addresses or names of ranges for the X data range and data ranges A–F.
   or
   To use a worksheet range you have set up especially for graphing, select the **Group Range** button, make selections in the Chart Ranges Group Range dialog box, then select **OK.** Skip step 7. (See "Notes" and "Options," below.)
7. To plot any of the graph data ranges against the second Y axis, select the **2nd Y** check box next to the Range text box.
8. Select **OK.**

• NOTES If you use the Group Range method of assigning data ranges in step 6, the worksheet range must be set up especially for graphing. Data ranges must correspond either to consecutive columns or rows in the worksheet. The first column (or row) will be assigned to the X data range. Columns (or rows) 2–7 will be assigned in sequence to data ranges A–F. If you select Columnwise assignment and specify a range that has only one column, the program makes it data range A. (See Figures III.6 and III.7.)

If you select Pie as the chart type, the first column (or row) will be used as pie-slice labels, and the second column (or row) will be data range A. A single pie chart has only one data range. However, data range B can be used to assign colors to pie slices. The color of each cell in the range will be assigned to the corresponding slice of the pie. (The data content of the cell is ignored. See Figures III.8 and III.9.)

By default, pie charts are generated with percent labels for each slice. To override this, assign a data range C that contains labels for the slices.

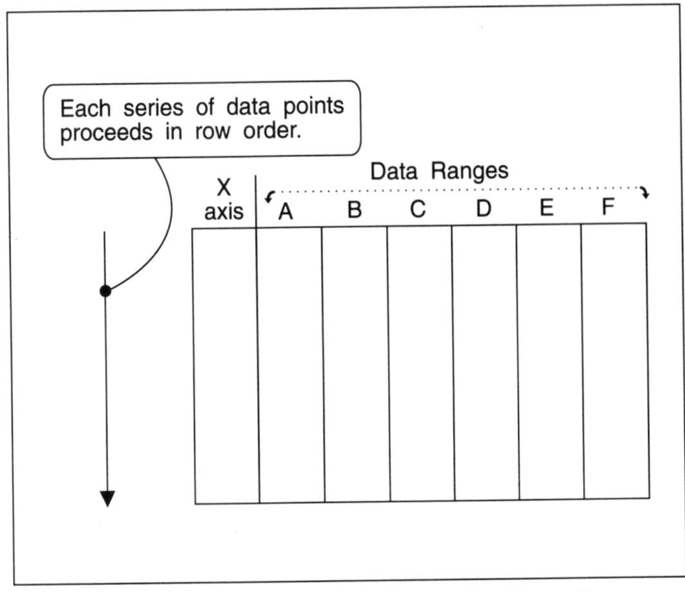

Figure III.6: Worksheet layout for Chart Ranges Group Range, columnwise

• **OPTIONS** In step 6, you can assign data ranges by selecting the Group Range button in the Chart Ranges dialog box, which assigns data for plotting from a specially designed worksheet range. (See "Notes," above.) Options in this dialog box are:

Divide into data ranges Subdivides the range to be graphed by columns (Columnwise) or by rows (Rowwise).

Range In the text box, enter the address or name of the worksheet range to be graphed.

See Also *Chart Options, Chart Type.* Part II: *Range Addressing, Range Name.*

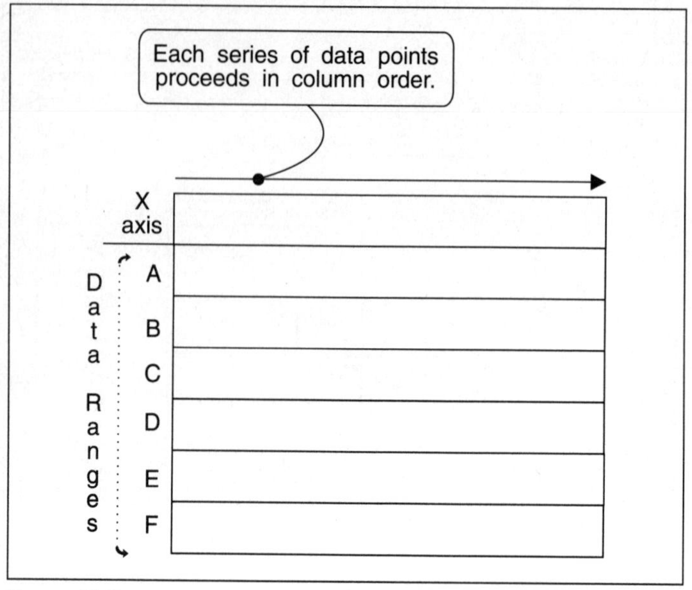

Figure III.7: Worksheet layout for Chart Ranges Group Range, rowwise

CHART TYPE

Permits you to set the chart type, or plotting method, for a chart or graph. Optionally, you can specify the orientation of axes and generate a table of values. SmartIcons are also available for quick selection of chart types.

To Select the Chart Type:

1. From the Main Menu bar, select **Graph.**
2. From the Graph pull-down, select **New** (for a new chart) or **View** (for an existing chart).

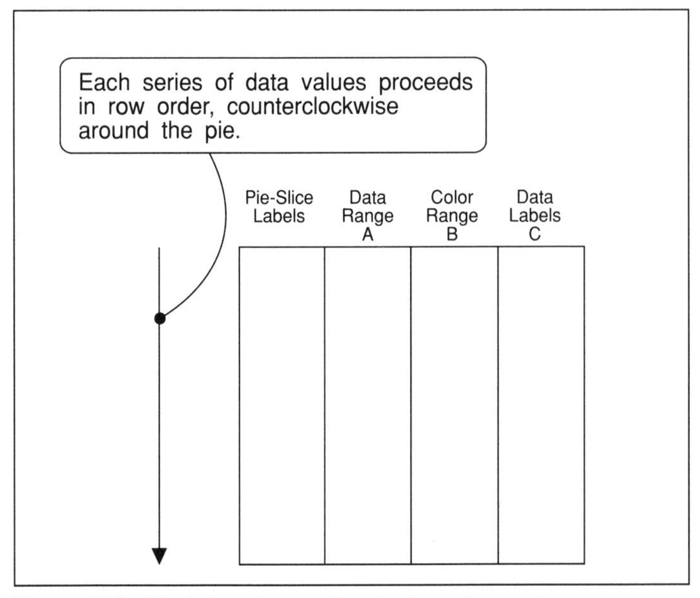

Figure III.8: Worksheet layout for pie chart data, columnwise

3. In the dialog box that appears, specify a graph name and select **OK.**
4. The Graph menu bar appears. Select **Chart.**
5. From the Chart pull-down, select **Type.**
6. In the Chart Type dialog box, select one of the types and the orientation of axes. (The default is Vertical unless you specifically select Horizontal.) (See "Options," below.)
7. If Bar is chosen, select one of the two icons to indicate how bars will be stacked or clustered. For Mixed, select one of the four icons displayed. For 3D Bar, select one of the three icons.
8. Optionally, to generate a table in the graph of data values for each graph data range, select the **Include Table of Values** check box.
9. Select **OK.**

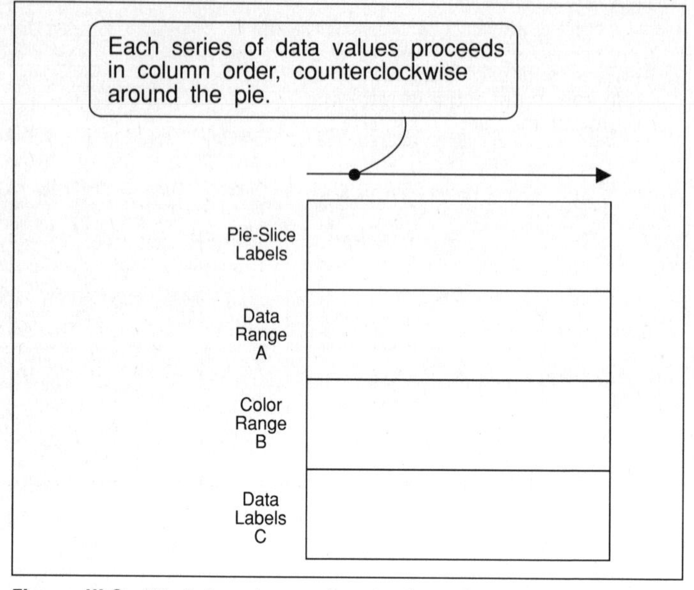

Figure III.9: Worksheet layout for pie chart data, rowwise

To Change Chart Type:

1. Select a graph window in the current file.
   or
   Follow steps 1–3 above.
3. From the palette of SmartIcons, select the icon for the chart type you want.
4. If you selected Mixed, perform step 6 above for each data range to be charted.
5. The current graph is converted to the new type and displayed.

• NOTES Each series of data items to be plotted is called a *data range* or *graph data range.* Data ranges are designated A–F and are linked to worksheet data ranges with the Chart Ranges command. The following graph types plot up to six ranges: Line, Area, Bar, XY,

HLCO, Mixed, 3D Line, 3D Area, and 3D Bar. Pie and 3D Pie types graph one data range as a segmented, circular area.

Graphing conventions normally plot time on the X axis and quantity (such as dollars or units) on the Y axis. Use Vertical orientation (the default) for most types of graphs unless you are plotting durations, or time spans, as horizontal bars.

Use line plots to show continuous variation and trends. Use bar charts to compare performance of different entities. Use area plots to emphasize volumes with trends. Use XY (scatter) charts to plot discrete points gathered through experimental or statistical means.

If a worksheet range is used to define the X axis and the labels are too long, the program automatically staggers the positions of the labels along the axis.

In stacked plotting, data ranges are layered on one another so that the Y values of each range are cumulative with respect to preceding ranges.

• OPTIONS Options in the Chart Types dialog box in step 6 include the following:

Types Select one radio button to determine the chart type, or plotting method. (See Figure III.10.)

Line Links data points with a continuous line. One line is plotted for each data range A–F. Optionally, a symbol is shown at each point. (See "Chart Options Lines.")

Area Links data points with a continuous line and shades the area beneath it with color and/or hatching. One area is plotted for each data range A–F.

Bar Shows Y data values as separate (clustered) bars or layered (stacked) bar segments. One bar or bar segment is plotted for each data range A–F.

Pie Plots *one* data range (usually A) as slices, or wedges, of a circular area, or pie.

XY Plots discrete points in a scatter chart. One type of symbol is plotted for each series of points in data ranges A–F.

HLCO Shows data ranges A–D as high, low, close, and open values respectively on a bar chart of stock prices. Data range E

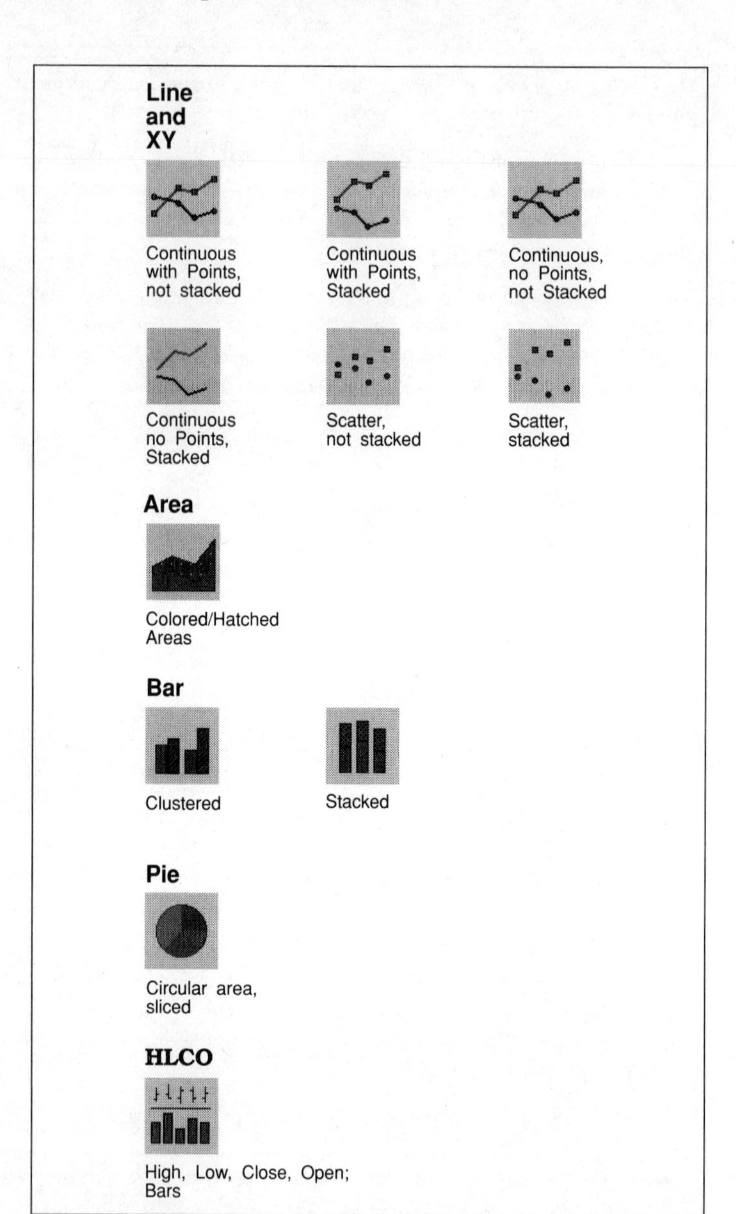

Figure III.10: Chart types and plotting styles

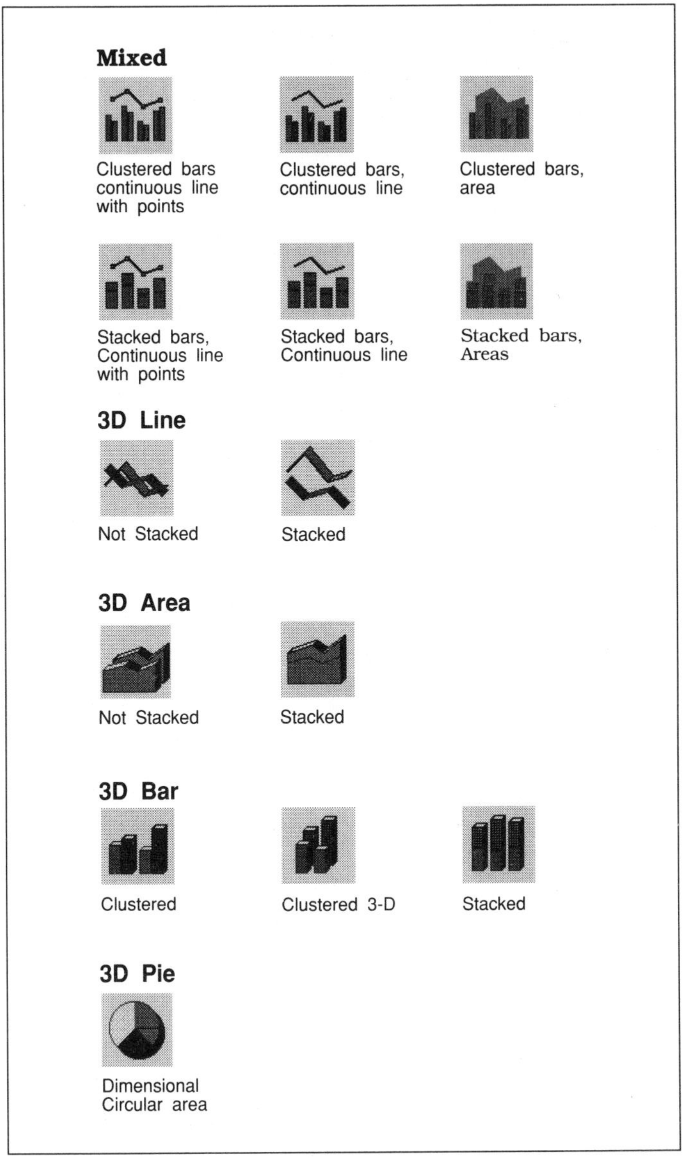

Mixed

Clustered bars continuous line with points

Clustered bars, continuous line

Clustered bars, area

Stacked bars, Continuous line with points

Stacked bars, Continuous line

Stacked bars, Areas

3D Line

Not Stacked

Stacked

3D Area

Not Stacked

Stacked

3D Bar

Clustered

Clustered 3-D

Stacked

3D Pie

Dimensional Circular area

Figure III.10: Chart types and plotting styles (continued)

is plotted as a series of bars beneath the HLCO area and is typically used to plot daily volume. Data range F is plotted as a line within the HLCO area and can be used for comparisons with other financial indicators, such as interest or monetary exchange rates.

Mixed Plots data ranges A–C as clustered or stacked bars and data ranges D–F as lines or areas.

3D Line Shows stacked or unstacked lines with a dimensional effect. (The lines look like ribbons.) One line is plotted for each data range A–F.

3D Area Similar to 3D Line, but with shaded (colored and/or hatched) areas between the line plots. One area is plotted for each data range A–F.

3D Bar Similar to Bar, but with a dimensional effect. (The bars look like blocks.) One bar or bar segment is plotted for each data range A–F.

3D Pie Similar to Pie, but with a dimensional effect on the circular area. One data range (usually A) is plotted.

Plot Style When you make a type selection, a set of icons appears in the dialog box for the plotting style to be used.

Line and XY styles Can be continuous with points, continuous without points, or scatter (points only).

Bar styles Can be clustered or stacked. Clustered shows a separate bar for each Y value in data ranges A–F for each X value, forming a cluster of bars at each X axis division. Stacked data ranges A–F are placed atop one another as segments of a single bar at each X axis division. (The bars look like stacks of building blocks.)

Mixed styles Include clustered bars with lines and points, clustered bars with lines, clustered bars with areas, stacked bars with lines and points, stacked bars with lines, and stacked bars with areas.

3D lines and areas Can be unstacked or stacked (cumulative among data ranges).

3D bars Can be clustered, stacked, or clustered in three dimensions. Instead of clustering bars next to one another, bars clustered in three dimensions are layered along the third dimension (a Z axis, in effect) at each X axis division.

Others Have only one plotting style: Area, Pie, HLCO, and 3D Pie.

Orientation Does not apply to Pie and 3D Pie chart types. For the other types, you can choose between:

Vertical The default, generates a vertical Y axis and horizontal X axis. This is the conventional plotting format for showing time (X) versus quantity (Y).

Horizontal Resets the plot orientation to show a vertical X axis and horizontal Y axis. If dual-Y plotting is done by selecting 2nd Y for any data range, the Y scale is shown along the bottom and the 2nd Y along the top of the plotting area.

Include Table of Values Generates a worksheet-style table with X values in the first row, A values in the second row, B values in the third row, and so on for all data ranges displayed in the graph. This option is not available for HLCO and XY graphs or for graphs in horizontal orientation.

See Also *Chart Axis, Chart Options, Chart Ranges. Appendix A: SmartIcons.*

DRAW ARROW

For annotating charts, draws a straight line segment (or connected segments) tipped with an arrowhead. Optionally, select the **arrow** icon from the set of SmartIcons instead.

The steps for drawing an arrow are identical to those for drawing lines, except that an arrowhead is added automatically at the endpoint. (See Figure III.11 and "Draw Line.")

See Also *Draw Line, Moving Objects, Rearrange Adjust Size, Selecting Objects, Style Color, Style Line. Appendix A: SmartIcons.*

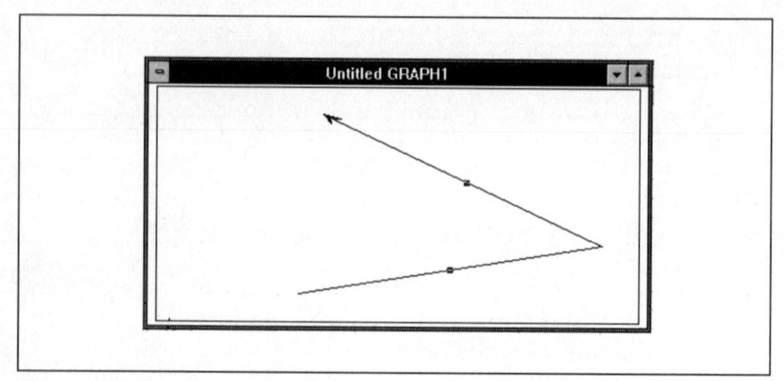

Figure III.11: An arrow, shown with the handles by which it can be manipulated

DRAW ELLIPSE

For annotating charts, draws an ellipse or circle. Optionally, select the **ellipse** icon from the set of SmartIcons instead. (See Figure III.12.)

To Draw an Ellipse or Circle:

1. From the Main Menu bar, select **Graph.**

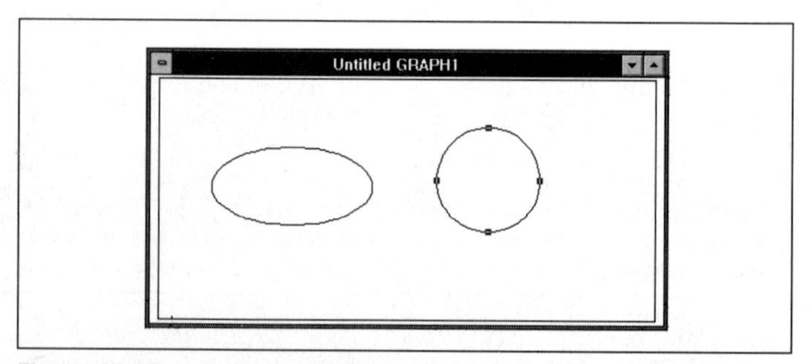

Figure III.12: An ellipse, shown with the handles by which it can be manipulated

2. From the Graph pull-down, select **New** (for a new chart) or **View** (for an existing chart).
3. In the dialog box that appears, specify a graph name and select **OK.**
4. The Graph menu bar appears. Select **Draw.**
   or
   Select the **ellipse** icon from the palette of SmartIcons, and skip step 5.
5. From the Draw pull-down, select **Ellipse.**
6. Move the pointer (drawing cursor) to the first corner of a box that will contain the ellipse. Anchor the point by dragging the mouse or pressing the **spacebar.**
7. Continue to drag the pointer, or press the arrow keys, stretching the reference box that will contain the ellipse, to the second corner and select it by releasing the mouse button or pressing ↵.

• NOTES To force a circle to be drawn, press the **Shift** key while anchoring the first corner and hold it down until you select the second corner of the box that will contain the circle.

To fill the area inside the ellipse or circle, select **Style Color Interior Fill** immediately *after* creating the object. (See "Selecting Objects.")

See Also *Moving Objects, Rearrange Adjust Size, Selecting Objects, Style Color. Appendix A: SmartIcons.*

DRAW FREEHAND

For annotating charts, draws a line that follows the pointer as you draw with the mouse or arrow keys. Optionally, select the **freehand line** icon from the set of SmartIcons instead. (See Figure III.13.)

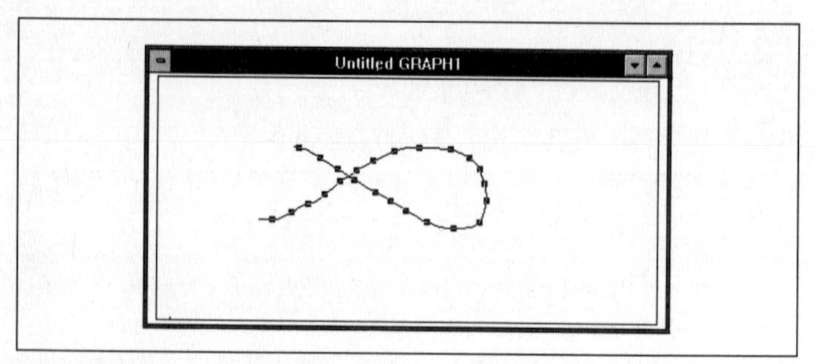

Figure III.13: A freehand line, shown with the handles by which it can be manipulated

To Draw a Freehand Line:

1. From the Main Menu bar, select **Graph.**
2. From the Graph pull-down, select **New** (for a new chart) or **View** (for an existing chart).
3. In the dialog box that appears, specify a graph name and select **OK.**
4. The Graph menu bar appears. Select **Draw.**

   or

   Select the **freehand line** icon from the palette of Smart-Icons, and skip step 5.
5. From the Draw pull-down, select **Freehand.**
6. Move the pointer (drawing cursor) to the first point and anchor it by dragging or by pressing the **spacebar.**
7. Continue to drag the pointer, or press the arrow keys, to trace the freehand line.
8. Finish the line by releasing the mouse button at the last point or by pressing ↵.

• NOTES To set line color, use **Style Color Line.** To control line style, width, arrowheads, and curvature, use **Style Line.** These Style commands should be used immediately *after* creating the object. (See "Selecting Objects.")

See Also *Draw Line, Moving Objects, Rearrange Adjust Size, Selecting Objects, Style Color, Style Line. Appendix A: SmartIcons.*

DRAW LINE

For annotating charts, draws a straight line segment (or series of connected segments). Optionally, select the **line** icon from the set of SmartIcons instead. (See Figure III.14.)

To Draw a Line:

1. From the Main Menu bar, select **Graph.**
2. From the Graph pull-down, select **New** (for a new chart) or **View** (for an existing chart).
3. In the dialog box that appears, specify a graph name and select **OK.**
4. The Graph menu bar appears. Select **Draw.**
   or
   Select the **line** icon from the palette of SmartIcons, and skip step 5.
5. From the Draw pull-down, select **Line.**

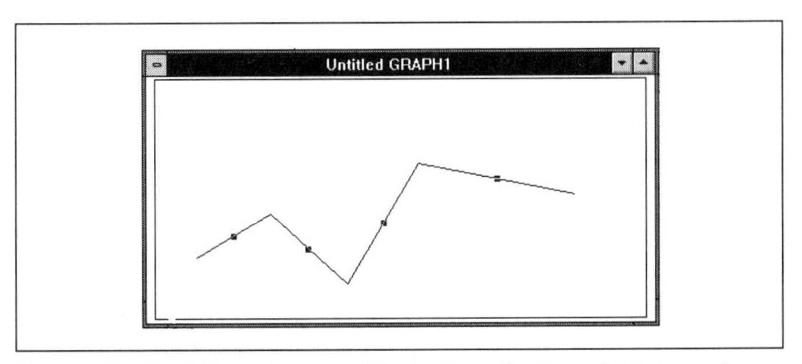

Figure III.14: A line, shown with the handles by which it can be manipulated

6. With the mouse or arrow keys, move the pointer (drawing cursor) to the first point and anchor it by clicking or pressing the **spacebar.**
7. Move the pointer to the second point and select it by clicking or pressing the **spacebar.**
8. Repeat step 7 for each point, or vertex, of the line.
9. Finish the line by double-clicking on the last point or pressing ↵.

• NOTES To undo the previous line segment, click the right mouse button or press **Esc.**

To force a line segment to follow the nearest 45-degree angle, press the **Shift** key while anchoring the first point and hold it down until you select the endpoint of the segment. This feature is especially useful for creating perpendicular lines.

To set line color, use **Style Color Line.** To control line style, width, arrowheads, and curvature, use **Style Line.** Use these Style commands immediately *after* creating the object. (See "Selecting Objects.")

See Also *Draw Arrow, Moving Objects, Rearrange Adjust Size, Selecting Objects, Style Color. Appendix A: SmartIcons.*

DRAW POLYGON

For annotating charts, draws polygons, or closed areas, which can be filled or hollow. Optionally, select the **polygon** icon from the set of SmartIcons instead. (See Figure III.15.)

To Draw a Polygon:

1. From the Main Menu bar, select **Graph.**

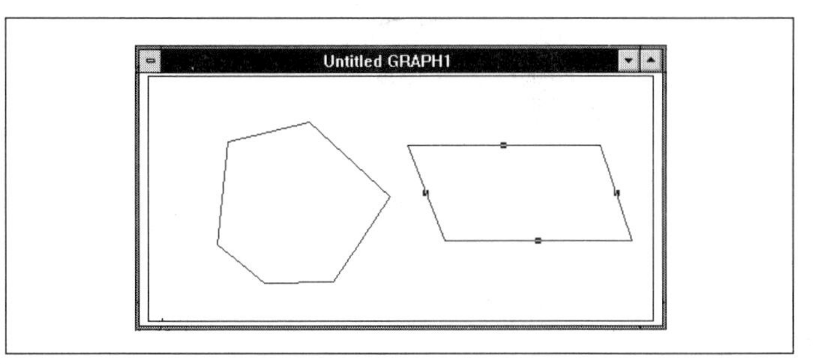

Figure III.15: A polygon, shown with the handles by which it can be manipulated

2. From the Graph pull-down, select **New** (for a new chart) or **View** (for an existing chart).
3. In the dialog box that appears, specify a graph name and select **OK.**
4. The Graph menu bar appears. Select **Draw.**
   or
   Select the **polygon** icon from the palette of SmartIcons, and skip step 5.
5. From the Draw pull-down, select **Polygon.**
6. Move the pointer (drawing cursor) to the first point and anchor it by clicking or pressing the **spacebar.**
7. Move the pointer to the second point and select it by clicking or pressing the **spacebar.**
8. Repeat step 7 for each point, or vertex of the polygon.
9. Finish the polygon by double-clicking on the last point or pressing ↵. The program automatically draws a line segment between the last and first points, closing the polygon.

• NOTES To draw four-sided polygons, such as squares and rectangles, use **Draw Rectangle** instead.

To undo the previous line segment, click the right mouse button or press **Esc.**

To force a line segment to follow the nearest 45-degree angle, press the **Shift** key while anchoring the first point and hold it down until you select the endpoint of the segment. This feature is especially useful for creating perpendicular edges. There is no special facility in 1-2-3 for drawing regular (equilateral) polygons.

To set the color of the polygon outline, use **Style Color Line.** To fill the area inside the polygon, select **Style Color Interior Fill.** Use these Style commands immediately *after* creating the object. (See "Selecting Objects.")

See Also *Draw Rectangle, Moving Objects, Rearrange Adjust Size, Selecting Objects, Style Color, Style Line. Appendix A: SmartIcons.*

DRAW RECTANGLE

For annotating charts, draws a rectangle or square, which can be filled or hollow. Optionally, select the **rectangle** icon from the set of SmartIcons instead. (See Figure III.16.)

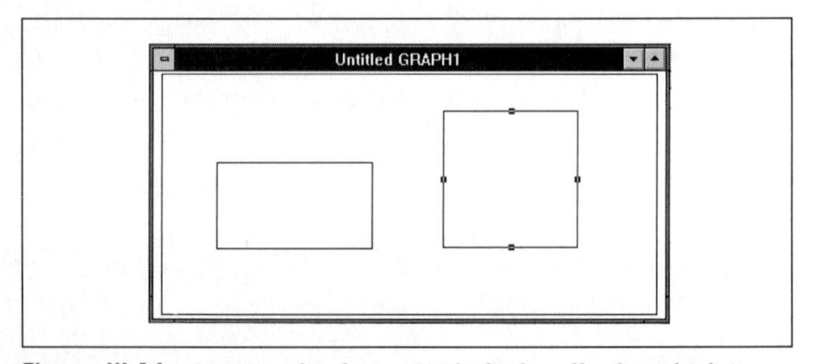

Figure III.16: A rectangle, shown with the handles by which it can be manipulated

To Draw a Rectangle or Square:

1. From the Main Menu bar, select **Graph.**
2. From the Graph pull-down, select **New** (for a new chart) or **View** (for an existing chart).
3. In the dialog box that appears, specify a graph name and select **OK.**
4. The Graph menu bar appears. Select **Draw.**
   or
   Select the **rectangle** icon from the palette of SmartIcons, and skip step 5.
5. From the Draw pull-down, select **Rectangle.**
6. Move the pointer (drawing cursor) to the first corner of the rectangle. Anchor the point by dragging or by pressing the **spacebar.**
7. Continue to drag the pointer to stretch the rectangle box to the second corner, and select it by releasing the mouse button.
   or
   Use the arrow keys to move the pointer to the second corner and press ↵.

• NOTES To force a square to be drawn, press the **Shift** key while you anchor the first corner and hold it down until you select the second corner.

To fill the area inside the rectangle, select **Style Color Interior Fill** immediately *after* creating the object. (See "Selecting Objects.")

See Also *Draw Polygon, Moving Objects, Rearrange Adjust Size, Selecting Objects, Style Color. Appendix A: SmartIcons.*

DRAW TEXT

Permits you to enter text annotations anywhere within a graph window. Optionally, use the **text** icon in the set of SmartIcons instead. (See Figure III.17.)

To Create Text:

1. From the Main Menu bar, select **Graph.**
2. From the Graph pull-down, select **New** (for a new chart) or **View** (for an existing chart).
3. In the dialog box that appears, specify a graph name and select **OK.**
4. The Graph menu bar appears. Select **Draw.**
   or
   Select the **text** icon from the palette of SmartIcons, and skip step 5.
5. From the Draw pull-down, select **Text.**
6. The Draw Text dialog box appears. Enter a text string in the New Text text box, and select **OK.**

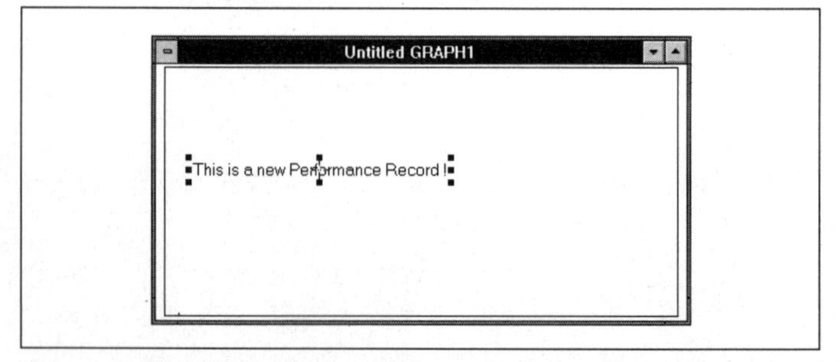

Figure III.17: A line of text, shown with the handles by which it can be manipulated

7. Move the pointer to position the text and select it by clicking or pressing ↵.

• NOTES Control text attributes through the Style commands **Font, Color,** and **Alignment.** Execute these commands immediately *after* creating an object. (See "Selecting Objects.")

Only text objects created with Draw Text or with the text icon can be selected and moved or manipulated with Graph commands.

To add titles, subtitles, and footnotes, use **Chart Headings** instead. For chart axis titles, use **Chart Axis X/Y/2ndY Options Axis Title.** Other useful alternatives are Chart Data Labels and Chart Legend.

See Also *Chart Axis, Chart Data Labels, Chart Headings, Chart Legend, Moving Objects, Rearrange Adjust Size, Selecting Objects, Style Alignment, Style Color, Style Font. Appendix A: SmartIcons.*

EDIT COPY

Places a copy of the current graph on the Clipboard (scratch-pad memory area in Windows). Use this command to move graphs and drawings between files, retrieving the data with **Edit Paste**.

To Copy a Graph to the Clipboard:

1. From the Main Menu bar, select **Graph.**
2. From the Graph pull-down, select **New** (for a new chart) or **View** (for an existing chart).
3. In the dialog box that appears, specify a graph name and select **OK.**
4. The Graph window menu appears. Select **Edit.**
5. From the Edit pull-down, select **Copy.**

• **NOTES** The copied data remain on the Clipboard until you perform Edit Copy again (either from the Graph window menu or the Main Menu) or Edit Cut (from the Main Menu).

When you use Edit Paste to retrieve data from the Clipboard into another application or file, a Dynamic Data Exchange (DDE) link is created, provided that the application supports DDE.

See Also *Edit Paste.* Part II: *Edit Copy, Edit Cut, Edit Link Options, Edit Paste. Appendix A: SmartIcons.*

EDIT DELETE/UNDELETE

Edit Delete removes a selected object or graph from the open graph document window. Edit Undelete restores an object or graph removed by the most recent Edit Delete command.

To Delete an Object or Graph:

1. In the graph window, select the object or graph to be removed.
2. From the Graph window menu, select **Edit.**
   or
   Select the **Delete** icon or press the **Del** key. Skip step 3.
3. From the Edit pull-down, select **Delete.**

To Restore a Deleted Object or Graph:

1. From the Graph window menu, select **Edit.**
   or
   Press the **Ins** key and skip step 2.
2. From the Edit pull-down select **Undelete.**

• **NOTE** To restore a deletion, perform **Edit Undelete** or press the **Ins** key before you use Edit Delete again.

See Also *Edit Select, Selecting Objects.* Part II: *Edit Clear, Edit Clear Special.*

EDIT REPLICATE

Duplicates, or generates multiple copies of, a selected object or graph in the open graph document window.

To Replicate an Object or Graph:

1. In the graph window, select the object or graph to be copied.
2. From the Graph window menu, select **Edit.**
   or
   Select the **Replicate** icon or press **Shift-Ins**. Skip step 3.
3. From the Edit pull-down, select **Replicate.**

• **NOTES** The program places another copy of the object or graph on top of the original. While the object is selected (handles showing), move the pointer to one of the handles and drag the object to another position in the graph document window.

If you do step 2 before selecting an object, the program displays the prompt **Select objects to duplicate** and the pointer becomes a cross-hairs, permitting you to perform the selection.

See Also *Edit Select, Moving Objects, Selecting Objects. Appendix A: SmartIcons.*

EDIT SELECT

Selects, or captures, objects or graphs for manipulation by other Graph window commands.

To Select an Object or Graph:

1. From the Graph window menu, select **Edit.**
2. From the Edit pull-down, select **Select.**
3. From the Select cascade, select **All, None,** or **Chart,** and skip steps 4–6.
   or
   Select **Cycle.**
4. In the Edit Select Cycle dialog box, select **Next** or **Previous** to cycle through the objects, including any graphs, in the open window.
5. When "hollow" handles appear around the desired object in the graph window, select **Select** in the dialog box.
6. Solid handles appear around the selected object. Select **OK.**
   or
   Select **Select** *again* to release the object, and repeat steps 4–6 to choose a different one.

• NOTES Objects can also be captured by pointing and clicking with the mouse. See "Selecting Objects."

When an object has been selected successfully, handles (small, solid squares) appear around it. You can move an object by dragging any of its handles. You can also change selected objects by executing commands included in the Layout, Rearrange, and Style pull-downs from the Graph window menu.

Objects are created in a succession of layers. The object created first is on the lowest layer, or is furthest back. Objects on top (or in front) obscure those beneath where they overlap. To change the order and thus the way objects overlay one another, use **Layout** commands.

Edit Select Cycle is particularly useful for sorting out multiple object copies that have been superimposed on one another by previous Edit Paste or Edit Replicate operations.

• OPTIONS Options in the Select cascade in step 3 are:

All Selects all objects in the current graph window, except graphs. Use this command to manipulate several objects as a group, as when moving graph annotations.

None Deselects, or releases, the object currently selected (surrounded by handles).

Chart Selects the entire graph in the current window, excluding any drawings or annotations you've made to it.

Cycle Automatically selects all objects in the current window, including any graphs, one by one. The objects can be selected in either of the following orders:

Next From the back forward, or in the order the objects were created.

Previous From the front backward, most recently created object first.

See Also *Layout Fall Back/Send Forward, Selecting Objects.*

FILE CLOSE

Closes the current graph window. Changes in a graph are saved automatically to the worksheet file on disk.

To Close the Current Graph Window:

1. From the Graph window menu, select **File.**
2. From the File pull-down, select **Close.**

See Also Part II: *File Close, File Save, File Save As.*

FILE EXIT

Performs the same actions as the Main Menu command File Exit: closes all document windows (graphs and worksheets), asks whether you wish to update the disk files, and ends the 1-2-3 session.

To Exit 1-2-3 from the Graph Menu:

1. From the Graph window menu, select **File.**
2. From the File pull-down, select **Exit.**
3. If you have made any changes to the open files, the File Exit dialog box appears. Select **Yes** (save all files to disk), **No** (abandon changes), or **Cancel** (return to the 1-2-3 session).

See Also Part II: *File Exit, File Save, File Save As.*

GRAPH ADD TO SHEET

A selection on the Main Menu bar, inserts a graph from another sheet in the file into the current worksheet and brings up the Graph window menu.

To Add a Graph to the Current Worksheet:

1. Move the pointer into a worksheet window and highlight the range that will hold the graph.
2. From the Main Menu, select **Graph.**

3. From the Graph pull-down, select **Add to Sheet.**
4. The Graph Add to Sheet dialog box appears with a list box containing all graph names in the current file. Select one of the graph names.
5. If you wish to override the range selected in step 1, specify a range name or address in the Range text box.
6. Select **OK.**

• NOTES To create a new graph from a range of data in the current sheet, use **Graph New** instead. To work with a graph that has already been inserted in the sheet or to look at a graph before it has been inserted, use **Graph View**.

To insert a graph from another active worksheet file, precede the graph name with a file reference (path and file name enclosed in double angle brackets <<>>) entered in the text box in step 4. To insert a graph that is stored externally as a separate .CGM or .PIC file, use **Graph Import.**

See Also *Graph Import, Graph New, Graph View.*

GRAPH GO TO

In the current worksheet window, moves the pointer to the first cell in the range that holds the named graph you choose. This command is useful for locating graphs that have been hidden.

To Move the Pointer to a Graph Range:

1. From the Main Menu, select **Graph.**
2. From the Graph pull-down, select **Go To.**
3. The Graph Go To dialog box appears with the names of all the current file's graphs in a list box. Select the graph name you want.

4. Select **OK.**

• NOTES This command merely locates the graph range in the worksheet. The worksheet window remains active. To work with a selected graph, use **Graph View**.

See Also *Graph View.*

GRAPH IMPORT

A selection on the Main Menu bar, reads a graph in an external file into the pointer location of the current worksheet. Imports either Computer Graphics Metafiles (.CGM extension) or Lotus graphs (.PIC extension, prior releases only).

To Import a Graph:

1. Highlight a range in the current sheet at which the graph will be inserted.
2. From the Main Menu, select **Graph.**
3. From the Graph pull-down, select **Import.**
4. In the Graph Import dialog box, specify the device, path, and file name that holds the graph.
5. Specify whether the file type is CGM or PIC by selecting one of the radio buttons.
6. If you wish to override the range selected in step 1, specify a range name or address in the Range text box.
7. Select **OK.**

• OPTIONS File types in step 5 are:

CGM The Computer Graphics Metafile format is a standard for exchange of graphic data among different computer graphic systems. Technically, the file is an object-oriented display list, which can be processed by graphics programs and intelligent output devices. Lotus Freelance Plus and Harvard Graphics (Software Publishing Corporation) are examples of business charting programs that can export CGM files.

PIC In 1-2-3 for Windows and in Release 3, graphs are saved in .FM3 files associated with worksheets. In prior releases (1A, 2.01, and 2.2), graphs can be saved separately with the .PIC extension by the /Graph Save command. In 1-2-3 for Windows, you can create a .PIC file by executing this command from the Classic menu. Note that this is a completely different file type from the .PIC bitmap files used by paint programs such as PC Paint (Mouse Systems Corporation).

See Also *Graph Add to Sheet.* Part I: *The Classic Menu.*

GRAPH NAME

A selection on the Main Menu bar, deletes a named graph in the current file or generates a table of named graphs and inserts it in the current sheet.

To Delete a Graph:

1. From the Main Menu, select **Graph.**
2. From the Graph pull-down, select **Name.**
3. From the Name cascade, select **Delete.**
4. The Graph Name Delete dialog box appears with all graph names in the current file shown in a list box. Select the name to delete.

   or

   Select **Delete All** to remove all graphs from the file, and skip steps 5 and 6.
5. Select **Delete.**

6. Repeat steps 4 and 5 to delete other graph names selectively from the file.
7. Select **OK.**

To Generate a Table of Graph Names:

1. Highlight a range in the current sheet that will hold the table.
2. From the Main Menu, select **Graph.**
3. From the Graph pull-down, select **Name.**
4. From the Name cascade, select **Paste Table.**
5. If you wish to override the range selected in step 1, in the Graph Name Paste Table dialog box, specify a range name or address in the Range text box.
6. Select **OK.**

• NOTES Graph Name Paste Table overwrites any data in the Selected range. The table has three columns: Graph name, Chart type, and Title. Each graph is a row, and the last row is left blank.

The dialog box in step 5 does not appear if you select a range large enough to hold the table in step 1.

See Also Part II: *Range Annotate, Range Name Delete, Range Name Paste Table.*

GRAPH NEW/VIEW

Selections from the Main Menu, permit you to open the document window for a new or existing graph in the current worksheet file. Executing either of these commands brings up the Graph window menu.

To Open a Graph:

1. For a new graph, highlight the range in the current worksheet that contains the data to be graphed.
   or
   For an existing graph, simply double-click on any cell in the range that contains it, and skip steps 2–6.
2. From the Main Menu, select **Graph.**
3. From the Graph pull-down, select **New** or **View.**
4. The Graph New (or View) dialog box appears. For a new graph, enter a name in the text box. For an existing graph, select a name from the list box.
5. For a new graph, if you wish to override the range selected in step 1, specify a range name or address in the Range text box.
6. Select **OK.**

• **NOTES** To create a worksheet range for graphing, make the first column the X range and put data ranges A–F in columns 2–7. For more information about plotting, see "Chart Type."

Graph View merely opens the selected graph window. It does not add the graph to the current sheet. To insert an existing graph in the sheet, use **Graph Add to Sheet** instead.

See Also *Chart Type, Graph Add to Sheet.*

GRAPH REFRESH

Recalculates, replots, and updates all graphs in the current worksheet file.

To Update Graphs:

1. Move the pointer into the worksheet window that contains the graphs to be updated.
2. From the Main Menu, select **Graph.**
3. From the Graph pull-down, select **Refresh.**

• **NOTES** This command is necessary only if you have turned off automatic recalculation with the Style Display Options command from the Graph window menu. The purpose of updating graphs is to make plots accurate after the corresponding worksheet data have been changed.

See Also *Style Display Options.*

GRAPH SIZE

A selection on the Main Menu, adjusts the size of the worksheet range that contains a graph.

To Resize a Graph Range:

1. Move the pointer to the range to be affected.
2. From the Main Menu, select **Graph.**
3. From the Graph pull-down, select **Size.**
4. In the Graph Size dialog box, select the name of the graph.
5. Specify new range limits in the Range text box.
6. Select **OK.**

• **NOTES** In step 5, the new range can be larger or smaller than the existing range, thus increasing or reducing the size of the graph as it is displayed in the worksheet.

To resize drawn objects, use **Rearrange Adjust Size**.

See Also *Rearrange Adjust Size, Worksheet Column Width.* Part II: *Worksheet Row Height.*

LAYOUT FALL BACK/SEND FORWARD

Moves a selected object backward or forward, changing the layer on which it appears.

To Change Object Layout:

1. Select the object to be moved ahead or behind other objects.
2. From the Graph window menu, select **Layout.**
   or
   Select either the **Send Forward** or **Fall Back** icon and skip step 3.
3. From the Layout pull-down, select **Send Forward** or **Fall Back.**

• **NOTES** Objects are created in a succession of layers. The object created first is on the lowest layer, or is furthest back. Objects on top (or in front) obscure those beneath where they overlap. Use **Edit Select Cycle** and **Next** or **Previous** to move among the layers for object selection. By default, a graph is placed in back, and other objects are drawn over it.

See Also *Edit Select, Selecting Objects. Appendix A: SmartIcons.*

LAYOUT LOCK/UNLOCK

Layout Lock freezes the position and attributes of a selected object or graph. Layout Unlock undoes the command.

To Lock/Unlock an Object:

1. Select the object to be affected.
2. From the Graph window menu, select **Layout.**
3. From the Layout pull-down, select **Lock** or **Unlock.**

• NOTES The handles of locked objects are shown as diamonds rather than squares.

One purpose of locking an object is to prevent accidental modifications. For example, you might lock a company logo so that it is always shown in the same position, size, and color.

See Also Part II: *Range Protect/Unprotect.*

MOVING OBJECTS

Simply select the object(s) to be moved, move the pointer to one of the handles, and drag the object to a new position. Handles are small, solid squares that surround an object once it has been selected.

See Also *Edit Select, Selecting Objects.*

REARRANGE ADJUST SIZE

Permits you to resize a selected object or graph.

To Resize an Object or Graph:

1. Select the object or graph to be resized.
2. From the Graph window menu, select **Rearrange.**
3. From the Rearrange pull-down, select **Adjust Size.**
4. A dotted box appears around the object. Stretch the box to the desired size.
5. Click or press ↵.

• **NOTES** You can distort the shape of an object with this command by stretching the reference box and changing its proportions. To prevent this, or to cause the object to retain its original shape, hold down the **Shift** key while performing steps 4 and 5.

See Also *Edit Select, Moving Objects, Selecting Objects.*

REARRANGE CLEAR

Undoes any previous Rearrange commands and restores the appearance of a selected object or graph.

To Cancel Rearrangement:

1. Select the object(s) to be affected.
2. From the Graph window menu, select **Rearrange.**
3. From the Rearrange pull-down, select **Clear.**

See Also *Chart Clear, Selecting Objects.*

REARRANGE FLIP

Creates a mirror-image of an object, flipping it horizontally or vertically (Figure III.18).

To Flip an Object:

1. Select the object(s) to be affected.

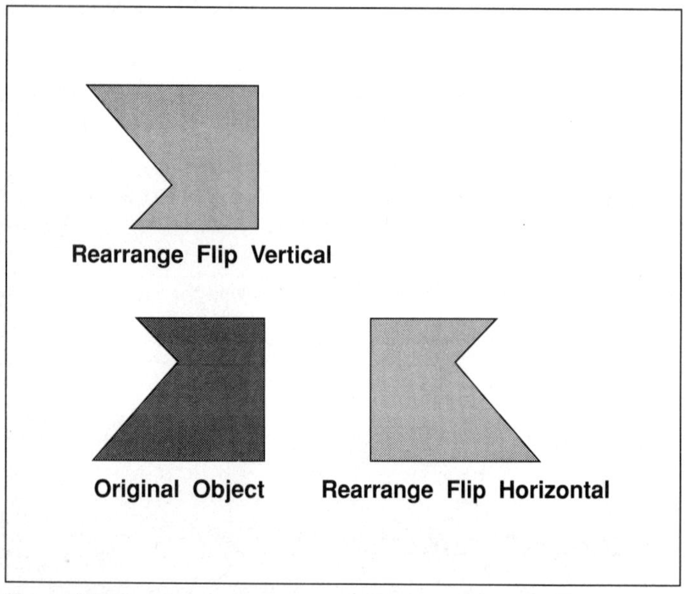

Figure III.18: Mirror images created with Rearrange Flip

2. From the Graph window menu, select **Rearrange.**
   or
   Select either the **Flip Horizontal** or **Flip Vertical** icon and skip steps 3 and 4.
3. From the Rearrange pull-down, select **Flip.**
4. From the Flip cascade, select **Horizontal** or **Vertical.**

See Also *Selecting Objects. Appendix A: SmartIcons.*

REARRANGE QUARTER-TURN/TURN

Rotate a selected object or graph, either continuously (Rearrange Turn) or by 90-degree increments (Rearrange Quarter-Turn). (See Figure III.19.)

To Rotate an Object:

1. Select the object to be affected.
2. From the Graph window menu, select **Rearrange.**
   or
   Select the **Turn** icon and skip step 3.
3. From the Rearrange pull-down, select **Quarter-Turn** and skip steps 4 and 5.
   or
   Select **Turn.**
4. If you selected Turn, a dotted box appears around the selected object, with a reference line indicating the current position. Use the mouse or the arrow keys to rotate the box and reference line to the desired position.
5. Click or press ↵.

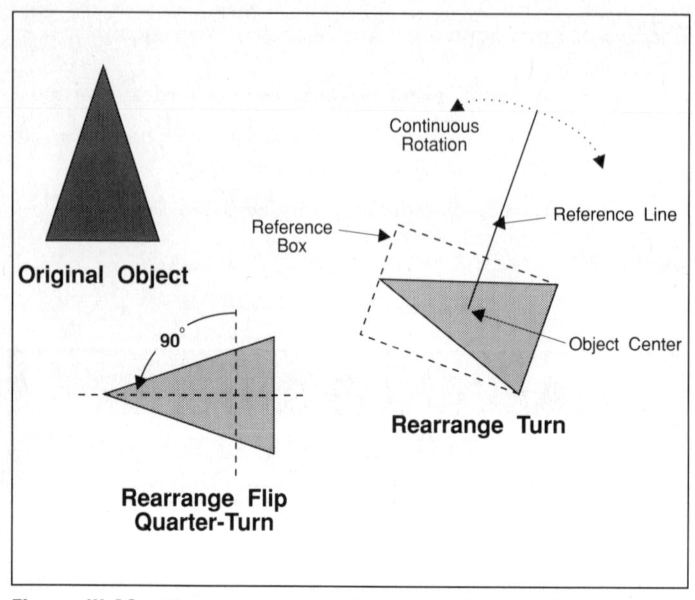

Figure III.19: Objects rotated by Rearrange Quarter-Turn and Rearrange Turn

• NOTES Use **Rearrange Quarter-Turn** if you want to make sure that the result will be precisely orthogonal, or perpendicular, to the position of the original object. The direction of rotation is counterclockwise.

See Also *Selecting Objects. Appendix A: SmartIcons.*

REARRANGE SKEW

Distorts a selected object or graph so that it appears to slant up or down (around its horizontal axis), or to the right or left (around its vertical axis). Affects both degree of slant and object size. (See Figure III.20.)

To Skew an Object:

1. Select the object to be affected.
2. From the Graph window menu, select **Rearrange.**
3. From the Rearrange pull-down, select **Skew.**
4. From the Skew cascade, select **Horizontal** or **Vertical**.
5. A dotted box appears around the selected object. Use the mouse or the arrow keys to adjust the size and slant of the reference box.
6. Click or press ↵.

See Also *Edit Select, Selecting Objects.*

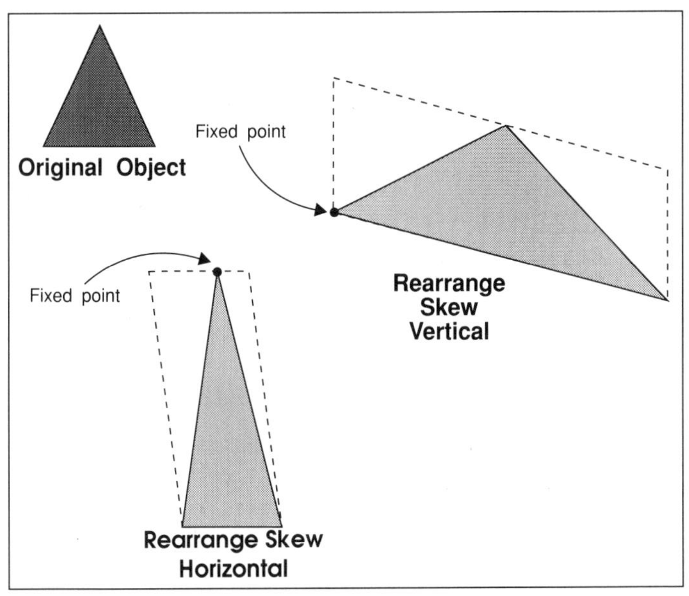

Figure III.20: Object slanted and sized with Rearrange Skew

SELECTING OBJECTS

Objects must be selected before they can be manipulated or changed by commands on the Graph window menu. An object that has been selected is surrounded by handles, or small, solid squares. Also, multiple objects can be selected in a single operation so that a command can be performed on them as a group.

To Select One Object with the Mouse:

1. Move the pointer to the edge of the object and click on it.
2. Handles appear around the object. If the handles appear around another object nearby instead, click again.
3. Repeat step 2 as the program cycles through all objects at that location until handles appear around the object you want.

To Select Several Objects at Once:

1. Drag a box that completely surrounds the objects to be selected, touching none of them.
2. Handles should appear around all objects that were contained in the box.

To Release Selected Objects:

- Move the pointer off the object and click.

To Release One of a Group of Selected Objects:

- Move the pointer to the object and click on it while pressing the **Shift** key.

• **NOTES** To select objects through the keyboard, use the **Edit Select** commands. These commands can also be performed with the mouse.

If its handles are in the shape of diamonds instead of squares, the object is locked, or protected from modification. You must use **Layout Unlock** before you can make changes.

Objects within graphs that are generated by Chart commands cannot be selected or manipulated individually.

See Also *Edit Select, Moving Objects.*

STYLE ALIGNMENT

Sets the justification of text created with the Draw Text command. The point of alignment in the graph window is the center of original text line.

To Align Text:

1. Select the text object(s), or line(s) of text, to be aligned.
2. From the Graph window menu, select **Style.**
3. From the Style pull-down, select **Alignment.**
4. In the Style Alignment dialog box, select **Left, Center,** or **Right.**
5. Select **OK.**

• **NOTES** If you do not select an object in step 1, the program asks you to select it after step 5.

See Also *Draw Text, Selecting Objects.* Part II: *Style Alignment.*

STYLE COLOR

For the current graph or a selected object, permits you to choose colors for text, drawn lines, object fill, and graph background.

To Select Graph Colors:

1. Select the object(s) to be recolored.
2. From the Graph window menu, select **Style.**
3. From the Style pull-down, select **Colors.**
4. In the Style Alignment dialog box, select colors for the Text, Line, Interior Fill, and Background drop-down boxes.
5. Select **OK.**

• NOTES See guidelines for matching colors and output types in "Style Color" in Part II. To set colors for plots, use **Chart Options Colors**.

When an object is created with one of the Draw commands, handles appear around it so that it can be manipulated. Use **Style Color** at this point to recolor the object.

If you do not select an object in step 1, the program asks you to select it after step 5.

• OPTIONS The following Select Colors options are available in the Style Color dialog box in step 4 (on a monochrome display, these are different shade patterns):

Text Can be black, white, red, green, blue, cyan, yellow, magenta, or hidden (H).

Line Can be black, white, red, green, blue, cyan, yellow, magenta, or hidden (H).

Interior fill Within solid objects such as ellipses, rectangles, and polygons, can be any one of 256 colors, including white, black, 14 shades of gray, and transparent (T).

Background Can be any one of 256 colors, including white, black, 14 shades of gray, and transparent (T).

See Also *Chart Options Colors, Edit Select, Selecting Objects*, Part II: *Style Color.*

STYLE DISPLAY OPTIONS

Sets various parameters affecting the display of graphs within worksheets.

To Set Graph Display Options:

1. From the Graph window menu, select **Style.**
2. From the Style pull-down, select **Display Options.**
3. In the Style Display Options dialog box, select check boxes for Graph Display on Sheet options and Show Grid Lines.
4. Select **OK.**

• OPTIONS Options in the dialog box in step 3 include the following:

Graph Display on Sheet Determines the manner of display for graphs within worksheet document windows and printouts.

Transparent Places the graph over the worksheet and lets the data in the sheet show through it.

Hidden Conceals the graph and displays it only as a shaded rectangle in the sheet. Graph details appear on printouts, however.

Updated automatically Recalculates plots automatically when the source data in the worksheet is updated.

Show Grid Lines Outlines the cells in the worksheet range that contains the graph. These lines are useful for positioning objects but are not visible when the graph is displayed in the worksheet window or in printouts. (These lines are not the same as the graph divisions set in Chart Borders/Grids.)

See Also Part II: *Window Display Options.*

STYLE FONT

Sets the font of text created with the Draw Text command and optionally resizes all text in the graph window.

To Set the Text Font:

1. Select the text object(s) to be affected.
2. From the Graph window menu, select **Style.**
3. From the Style pull-down, select **Font.**
4. In the Style Font dialog box, select one of the previously installed font names/sizes in the Fonts list box.
5. If you wish, resize all text in the current graph window by entering a value from 1–1000 percent in the Magnify all Fonts text box.
6. Select **OK.**

• **NOTE** The first font shown in the list box in step 4 is the default font for the worksheet file. (See "Style Font" in Part II.)

If you do not select an object in step 1, the program asks you to select it after step 6.

See Also Part II: *Draw Text, Edit Select, Selecting Objects, Style Font. Appendix D: Adobe Type Manager.*

STYLE LINES

For a selected object, sets style options for lines drawn with the Draw Lines command, including arrows, lines, the outlines of ellipses, freehand lines, polygons, and rectangles.

To Set Line Styles:

1. Select the object to be affected.
2. From the Graph window menu, select **Style.**
3. From the Style pull-down, select **Lines.**
4. In the Style Lines dialog box, select options in the Line drop-down box, as well as one of the options for smoothing.
5. Optionally, select one or both of the Add Arrowheads check boxes.
6. Select **OK.**

• **NOTE** Changing line smoothing can actually change the apparent object type. For example, selecting None for the smoothing of an ellipse transforms it into a rectangle. Changing a rectangle to Medium smoothing causes it to become an ellipse.

If you do not select an object in step 1, the program asks you to select it after step 6.

• **OPTIONS** The following options are available in the Style Lines dialog box in step 4:

Line Has two drop-down boxes:

Style Select one of six styles, including solid, two dashed styles, dotted, and two dashed-and-dotted styles.

Width Select one of five line widths, from thin to thick.

Add Arrowheads Places or removes an arrowhead at either or both:

Start of line Point of origin.

End of line Endpoint.

Smoothing Select one of the radio buttons to control line curvature:

None Straight line segments connect the points; no smoothing applied.

Tight Bends are curved, but sharply.

Medium Bends are made gradual.

See Also *Draw (Object Type), Edit Select, Selecting Objects.*

TOOLS SMARTICONS

Controls the display of the palette of SmartIcons graph tools and permits you to select and/or customize icons. (See "Tools SmartIcons" in Part II and Appendix A: "SmartIcons.")

WINDOW CASCADE/TILE

Control the display of multiple graph document windows as either cascades (stepped overlays) or tiles (side-by-side). (See "Window Cascade/Tile" in Part II.)

WINDOW ENLARGE/ FULL/REDUCE/ZOOM

Control the display of graphs and drawn objects within the current graph window. (None of these commands affect the appearance of the graph in the worksheet display or in outputs.)

To Control Your View of a Graph:

1. From the Graph window menu, select **Window.**
   or
   Press the appropriate control key: + (for Enlarge) or @ (for Zoom). Skip step 2.
2. From the Window pull-down, select the action to be performed: **Enlarge** or **Zoom.**
3. If you selected Enlarge, you can move around in the graph by adjusting the scroll bars at the edges of the window.
   or
   If you selected Zoom, move the pointer to one corner and drag a reference box in the window to indicate a portion of the graph to be enlarged. You can move around in the graph by adjusting the scroll bars.
4. If necessary, repeat Enlarge or Zoom operations (as many as four more times) to magnify the view further.
5. Select **Window Reduce** or press the minus key (–) to reverse previous Enlarge commands in steps.
   or
   Select **Window Full** or press the asterisk key (*) to restore the full-sized graph in the window.

• **NOTE** Use **Window Enlarge** and **Window Zoom** to magnify your view of the graph window to work in finer detail when you are making annotations with Draw commands and when you are moving or resizing objects.

WINDOW *FILENAME*

Permits you to switch to any of the currently open document windows, just as its Main Menu counterpart. (See "Window *Filename*" in Part II.)

Part Four

@Functions

@Functions calculate formulas, or perform algorithms, using data values you specify in formula syntax as *arguments.* Each @function has its own syntax, typically:

@FunctionName by itself, with no arguments

or

@FunctionName (*Argument1,Argument2,..,ArgumentN*)

Parentheses, where shown, are mandatory in @formula syntax. An @function and its arguments cannot exceed 512 characters in any given worksheet cell.

Entries in this section give @function names, followed by argument syntax and definitions. Optional arguments, which can be omitted, are enclosed in brackets [ ]. (Do not use brackets in @function syntax.)

DATABASE @FUNCTIONS

In database tables in worksheets and external database systems, perform queries and statistical analyses. (In 1-2-3, a *database table* is a range that contains one column for each field of a typical database record, ordered from left to right in the order the fields appear in the records. The top row in the table contains column-heading labels that are used as field names. Column widths correspond to field lengths, and cell formatting controls data typing.)

All database @functions except @dquery have the following syntax:

@FunctionName(*InputRange, FieldName, CriteriaRange***)**

where

- *InputRange* is the location of the database table (range address or name).
- *FieldName* is the name, offset number, or cell address of the field in the table to be searched.
- *CriteriaRange* is the range address/name containing data values to be tested by the @function.

Example:

@davg(A5..G20,4,J4..J5)

The database @functions and their syntax include the following:

@davg(*InputRange,FieldName,CriteriaRange***)** Determines the average of data values that meet the criteria range in the field.

@dcount(*InputRange,FieldName,CriteriaRange***)** Counts all cells in the field that contain data, excluding blank cells, and that meet the criteria.

@dget(*InputRange,FieldName,CriteriaRange***)** Searches for and retrieves a data item (value or label) that meets the criteria.

@dmax(*InputRange,FieldName,CriteriaRange***)** Retrieves the greatest value that meets the criteria in the field.

@dmin(*InputRange,FieldName,CriteriaRange*) Retrieves the least value that meets the criteria in the field.

@dquery(*ExternalCommand[,ExternalArguments]*) Lets you use a data query function (*ExternalCommand*) of an external database system and places its result in a criteria range. Consult the database system's documentation for required arguments, and use valid argument separators, such as commas, in multiple arguments.

@dstd(*InputRange,FieldName,CriteriaRange*) Calculates the *population* standard deviation of values in a list, or field that meets the criteria. Standard deviation is the degree to which values in a list vary from the mean. The population standard deviation tests all values in the list.

@dstds(*InputRange,FieldName,CriteriaRange*) Same as @dstd, but calculates the *sample* standard deviation. The sample standard deviation tests only a portion, or sample, of items in a long list.

@dsum(*InputRange,FieldName,CriteriaRange*) Returns the sum of all values that meet the criteria in the field.

@dvar(*InputRange,FieldName,CriteriaRange*) Determines the *population* variance of values that meet the criteria in a field. Variance is the degree to which values in a list vary from the mean. The population variation tests all values in the list.

@dvars(*InputRange,FieldName,CriteriaRange*) Same as @dvar, except determines the *sample* variance, based on a portion, or sample, of a long list.

DATE AND TIME @FUNCTIONS

Calculate dates and times based either on arguments you specify or on the current value in your computer system's clock/calendar. Date and time values you use as arguments must be integers or cell addresses/names that contain integers. Dates and times entered as text strings, where permitted, must be in one of the valid 1-2-3 formats.

@d360(*StartDate,EndDate*) Based on a 360-day year, calculates the interval between two date numbers (see "@date").

@date(*Year,Month,Day*) Calculates the date number (value from 1–73050, representing 1/1/1900–12/31/2099) for the calendar date.

@datevalue("*DateString*") Converts a date expressed as a text string into a date number (see "@date").

@day(*DateNumber*) Extracts from a date number (see "@date") only the day of the month (an integer from 1–31).

@days360(*StartDate,EndDate*) Similar to @d360, but uses a standard set by the Securities Industry Association.

@hour(*TimeNumber*) Extracts from a time number (see "@now," "@time," "@timevalue") only the hour of the 24-hour day (0–23).

@minute(*TimeNumber*) Extracts from a time number (see "@time") only the minutes value (0–59).

@month(*DateNumber*) Extracts from a date number (see "@date") only the month of the year (1–12).

@now Converts the value in your computer's clock/calendar to a date number (see "@date") and a time number (see "@time").

@second(*TimeNumber*) Extracts from a time number (see "@time") only the seconds value (0–59).

@time(*Hour,Minutes,Seconds*) Converts the time argument to a time number (0–.99988, representing 12:00:00AM–11:59:59PM).

@timevalue("*TimeString*") Converts a time expressed as a text string into a time number (see "@time").

@today Converts the value in your computer's clock/calendar to a date number (see "@date").

@year(*DateNumber*) Extracts from a date number (see "@date") only the year (0–199, representing 1900–2099).

FINANCIAL @FUNCTIONS

Apply formulas for investment analysis, including capital budgeting, ordinary annuities, and single-sum compound interest. Interest values used as arguments must not equal zero and must be greater than –1. Arguments can be numeric values or cell addresses/names.

@cterm(*FixedInterest,FutureValue,PresentValue*) Calculates the term, or number of compounding periods, during which an investment will grow, assuming a fixed rate of interest.

@ddb(*Cost,SalvageValue,UsefulLife,Period*) Using the double declining balance method, calculates the depreciation allowance for an asset (*Cost* >= *SalvageValue*, *UsefulLife* > 2, *Period* >= 1).

@fv(*PaymentAmount,FixedInterest,Term*) Calculates an investment's future value, based on payments of equal amounts.

@irr(*EstPercent,Range*) Calculates the internal rate of return of proceeds from cash flow in *Range.* (*EstPercent* must be a decimal 0–1, representing 0–100 percent estimated rate of return.)

@npv(*FixedInterest,Range*) Calculates the net present value (a discount for the time value of money) of a future series of values (*Range*) by a fixed rate of interest.

@pmt(*Principal,FixedInterest,Term*) Calculates the required payment amount for a loan.

@pv (*PaymentAmount,FixedInterest,Term*) Calculates an investment's present value, based on payments of equal amounts.

@rate(*FutureValue,PresentValue,Term*) Calculates the required rate of fixed interest that yields a desired future value of an investment, compounded over the specified term.

@sln(*Cost,SalvageValue,UsefulLife*) Calculates the allowance for straight line depreciation of an asset.

@syd(*Cost,SalvageValue,UsefulLife,Period*) Using the sum-of-the-years'-digits method, calculates the depreciation allowance for an asset (*Cost* ≥ *SalvageValue, UsefulLife* ≥ 1, *Period* ≥ 1).

@term(*PaymentAmount,FixedInterest,FutureValue*) Calculates the investment term required to reach a desired future value, based on payments of equal amounts.

@vdb(*Cost,SalvageValue,UsefulLife,StartPeriod,EndPeriod*) Using the variable-rate declining balance method, calculates the depreciation allowance for an asset (*Cost* ≥ *SalvageValue; UsefulLife* > 0; *StartPeriod* < *EndPeriod*, both decimals for fractions of years).

LOGICAL @FUNCTIONS

Perform Boolean, or logical, comparisons of values and return the result as either True (1) or False (0).

@false Generates the value 0.

@if(*Condition,FirstResult,SecondResult*) Performs a logical test *Condition*, such as X>Y. If true, *FirstResult* is returned; if false, *SecondResult*. *FirstResult* and *SecondResult* can be formulas, values, strings, or the cell addresses/names that contain them. Enclose strings in quotation marks ("").

@isaaf("*FunctionName*") Tests for *FunctionName* as the valid name of an add-in @function. Enclose *FunctionName* in quotation marks ("") and omit the @ symbol.

@isapp("*ApplicationName*") Checks whether the add-in program *ApplicationName* has been loaded into memory with Tools Add-In Load. Enclose *ApplicationName* in quotation marks ("") and omit any file extension.

@iserr(*ValueReference*) Tests whether the current value of *ValueReference* is ERR (error condition). *ValueReference* can be a formula, data value, cell address/name, text string, or condition statement (X>Y).

@isna(*ValueReference*) Tests whether the current value of *ValueReference* is NA (not available). *ValueReference* can be a formula, data value, cell address/name, text string, or condition statement (X>Y).

@isnumber(*ValueReference*) Tests whether the current value of *ValueReference* is a data value, ERR (error condition), NA (not available), or blank. The result is false if *ValueReference* is a formula or label. *ValueReference* can be a formula, data value, cell address/name, text string, or condition statement (X>Y).

@isrange(*Range*) Tests whether *Range* (address or name) is defined as a valid range in the worksheet.

@isstring(*ValueReference*) Tests whether the current value of *ValueReference* is text or a label. The result is false if *ValueReference* is a data value, ERR (error condition), NA (not available), or blank. *ValueReference* can be a formula, data value, cell address/name, text string, or condition statement (X>Y).

@true Generates the value 1.

MATHEMATICAL @FUNCTIONS

Perform arithmetic operations or mathematical functions on numeric values. Arguments can be numbers or cell addresses/names that contain numbers. In general, trigonometric functions require angle values expressed in radians. (To convert degrees to radians, multiply by @pi and divide by 180.)

@abs(*N*) Returns the absolute value (a positive number) of *N*.

@acos(*CosineValue*) Calculates the arc cosine (in radians), or inverse cosine, of the cosine of an angle.

@asin(*SineValue*) Calculates the arc sine (in radians), or inverse sine, of the sine of an angle.

@atan(*TangentValue*) Calculates the arc tangent (in radians), or inverse tangent, of the tangent of an angle.

@atan2(*Tangent2Value*) Calculates the arc tangent (in radians), or inverse tangent, of the tangent Y/X of an angle. Y and X are the lengths of any two sides of a triangle ($X \neq 0$).

@cos(*AngleValue*) Calculates the cosine of an angle that is expressed in radians.

@exp(*ExponentValue*) Raises the constant e to the power *ExponentValue* ($e \cong 2.718282$, $-11355.1371 < ExponentValue < 11356.5234$).

@int(*RealNumber*) Returns the integer (whole-number) component of *RealNumber.*

@ln(*N*) Calculates the natural logarithm (base e) of N.

@log(*N*) Calculates the common logarithm (base 10) of N.

@mod(*M/N*) Calculates the remainder (modulus) of dividing M by N ($N \neq 0$).

@pi Generates the constant π, or the ratio of a circle's circumference to its diameter ($\pi \cong 3.14159$).

@rand Generates a random decimal value from 0–1, calculated to 17 decimal places.

@round(*RealValue,Power*) Rounds the number *RealValue* to the nearest coefficient (multiple) of the *Power* of 10 ($-100 < Power < 100$).

@sin(*AngleValue*) Calculates the sine of an angle that is expressed in radians.

@sqrt(*N*) Calculates the positive square root of a positive value N.

@tan(*AngleValue*) Calculates the tangent of an angle that is expressed in radians.

SPECIAL @FUNCTIONS

Report the contents of cells in a worksheet.

Lookup tables, used with some special @functions, are specially constructed ranges that either have labels in the first column/row or values in ascending order.

@@(*CellReference*) Reports the contents of a cell address/ name. *CellReference* can also be a formula that generates a cell address/name.

@cell("*Attribute*",*RangeReference*) Reports on the attributes of the first cell in the specified range address/name. The Attribute argument must be one of the following keywords, enclosed in quotation marks: ADDRESS, COL, COLOR, CONTENTS, COORD, FILENAME, FORMAT, PARENTHESES, PREFIX, PROTECT, ROW, SHEET, TYPE, or WIDTH.

@cellpointer("*Attribute*") Reports on the attributes (see "@cell") of the current cell (pointer location).

@choose(*N,List*) Retrieves the *N*th item in a list. List is a range that holds a group of items with argument separators.

@cols(*Range*) Counts the number of columns in *Range.*

@coord(*SheetNumber,ColumnNumber,RowNumber,Absolute*) Generates a cell address/name from the worksheet number, column number (convert letters to numbers), and row number. *Absolute* (1–8) determines variations of absolute, mixed, or relative references.

@err Generates the value ERR (error condition).

@hlookup(*MinValue,Range,RowNumber*) Returns the nearest-match contents (based on *MinValue*) of a cell in specified row of a horizontal (rowwise) lookup table *Range.* Depending on the data type in the first column of the table, *MinValue* can be either a value or a string (enclosed in quotation marks).

@index(*Range,ColumnNumber,RowNumber*[,*SheetNumber*]) Reports the contents of the cell specified by the range address/name and offsets *ColumnNumber, RowNumber,* and (optionally) *SheetNumber.* (Convert column letters to numbers, offset by the starting column.)

@info("*ReportCode*") Reports on program status according to the *ReportCode*, or keyword, which must be enclosed in quotation marks: DBRETURNCODE, DBDRIVERMESSAGE, DBRECORDCOUNT, DIRECTORY, MEMAVAIL, MODE, NUMFILE, ORIGIN, OSRETURNCODE, OSVERSION, RECALC, RELEASE, SYSTEM, or TOTMEM.

@na Generates the value NA (not available).

@rows(*Range*) Counts the number of rows in *Range.*

@sheets(*Range*) Counts the number of worksheets in *Range.*

@solver("*StatusCode*") Reports on the status of the Solver program according to any one of the following *StatusCode* keywords: CONSISTENT, DONE, MOREANSWERS, NEEDGUESS, NUMANSWERS, OPTIMAL, PROGRESS, or RESULT.

@vlookup(*MinValue,Range,ColumnNumber*) Returns the nearest-match contents (based on *MinValue*) of a cell in specified column of a vertical (columnwise) lookup table *Range.* Depending on the data type in the first row of the table, *MinValue* can be either a value or a string (enclosed in quotation marks).

STATISTICAL @FUNCTIONS

Analyze and compile statistics about items in lists. Wherever the argument List is required, a range address/name containing a list may be used. A list, whether included in the argument itself or in a specified range, contains a series of values with argument separators.

@avg(*List*) Calculates the average of values in the list.

@count(*RangeList*) Counts the number of nonblank cells in the ranges listed in *RangeList* (a series of range references with argument separators).

@max(*List*) Returns the maximum, or highest, value in the list.

@min(*List*) Returns the minimum, or least, value in the list.

@std(*List*) Calculates the population standard deviation (see "@dstd").

@stds(*List*) Calculates the sample standard deviation (see "@dstds").

@sum(*List*) Returns the sum, or total, of values in the list.

@sumproduct(*RangeList*) For each position in a set of matched ranges (range references with argument separators), first multiplies the values, then calculates their sum.

@var(*List*) Calculates the population standard variance (see "@dvar").

@vars(*List*) Calculates the sample standard variance (see "@dvars").

STRING @FUNCTIONS

Apply transformations to text strings. LMBCS codes refer to the Lotus MultiByte Character Set. In general, strings can be string values enclosed in quotation marks, formulas that generate label values, or cell addresses/names that contain strings.

@char(*IntegerValue*) Returns the LMBCS equivalent of an integer.

@code(*String*) Returns the LMBCS code of the first character in *String*.

@exact(*FirstString,SecondString*) Compares two strings and returns True (1) if they match and False (0) if they differ.

@find(*DesiredString,LongString,Position*) Searches for a string (*DesiredString*) within a longer string (*LongString*), beginning at a specified character *Position* (integer). Returns the character position of the first character in the matching string.

@left(*String,N*) Returns the first *N* characters in *String*, counting from its left end.

@length(*String*) Counts the number of characters in *String*.

@lower(*String*) Converts all characters in *String* to lowercase.

@mid(*String,Position,N*) Returns *N* consecutive characters from *String*, beginning at the specified character *Position*.

@n(*Range*) Returns the numeric value contained in the first cell in *Range*. If non-numeric, returns a value of 0.

@proper(*String*) Makes the first character in *String* a capital letter and the rest lowercase.

@repeat(*String,N*) Duplicates the *String* value *N* times.

@replace(*InitialString,Position,N,InsertString*) In *InitialString*, starting at *Position*, replaces N characters with *InsertString*. If N = 0, the insertion is made without deleting any characters.

@right(*String*) Returns the last *N* characters in *String*, counting from its right end.

@s(*Range*) Returns the value in the first cell in *Range* as a label.

@string(*Number,N*) Converts a number to a label with *N* decimal places ($0 \leq N \leq 15$).

@trim(*String*) Deletes unnecessary space characters from *String*, including leading, trailing, and multiple internal consecutive spaces.

@upper(*String*) Converts all characters in *String* to capitals, or uppercase.

@value(*String*) Converts numeric digits that were entered as label data into a numeric value.

Appendix A

SmartIcons

SmartIcons are graphic buttons you click on with the mouse to trigger 1-2-3 commands quickly, bypassing the menu system. Different sets, or *palettes,* of SmartIcons are available for the Main (Worksheet) Menu, Graph window, and related commands.

A table of SmartIcons and their actions can be found on the inside front cover of this book.

To See an Explanation of an Icon:

1. Move the pointer to the icon in the current palette.
2. Click and hold the *right* mouse button.
3. An explanation appears at the top of the screen.

To Arrange the Icons on the Screen:

1. From either the Main Menu or Graph menu bar, select **Tools.**
2. From the Tools pull-down, select **SmartIcons.**
3. In the Palette Position dialog box, select the position on the screen at which the icon palette will be displayed: **Left, Right, Top, Bottom,** or **Floating.**
   or
   Select the **Hide Palette** check box to suppress display of the palette.
4. Select **OK.**
5. If you selected Floating in step 3, drag the palette to a desired position on the screen anytime during your work session.

To Select Different Icons:

1. From either the Main Menu or Graph menu bar, select **Tools.**
2. From the Tools pull-down, select **SmartIcons.**
3. In the Tools SmartIcons dialog box, select **Customize.**
4. In the Tools SmartIcons Customize dialog box, delete an icon in the Current Palette box by clicking on it and then selecting **Remove.**
5. Add an icon by clicking on it in the Standard Icons box and then selecting **Add.**
6. Select **OK.**

To Create New Icons:

1. From either the Main Menu or Graph menu bar, select **Tools.**
2. From the Tools pull-down, select **SmartIcons.**
3. In the Tools SmartIcons dialog box, select **Customize.**
4. In the Tools SmartIcons Customize dialog box, select a button for the new icon from the Custom Icons box.
5. Select **Assign Macro.**
6. In the Tools SmartIcons Customize Assign Macro dialog box, enter in the Range text box the entire address or name of the range that contains the macro.
7. Select **Get Macro.** The macro should appear in the Macro list box.
8. Select **OK.**
9. The Tools SmartIcons Customize dialog box reappears. Select **Add** to add the new icon to the current palette.
10. Select **OK.**

• NOTES In the Tools SmartIcons Customize dialog box, you can see an explanation of an icon when you select it from the Standard Icons, Current Palette, or Custom Icons box. The icon's action is shown in the Description information box.

If you select more than 26 icons for the current palette, specify **Floating** arrangement so that you can see them all.

Icon buttons for the Main Menu are stored as bitmap files (.BMP extension) in the subdirectory \SHEETICO. Graph menu icons are stored in \GRAPHICO. Any .BMP files in these directories will appear in the corresponding Custom Icons box when you select Tools SmartIcons Customize. Additional icon bitmap files and predefined macros are available from third-party vendors.

You can create your own icons with any graphics or paint program that generates bitmap files in .BMP format, including Windows Paintbrush. To make new icons quickly, use the file SAMPLE.BMP in the icon subdirectories as a template.

Once you've created a new icon bitmap, use **Tools SmartIcons Customize Assign Macro** to specify its action.

A listing of macro commands and their arguments is given in Appendix B. When used with SmartIcon macros, subroutine calls, branches, and branches created by the macro command **onerror** must refer to macros in the current worksheet.

Appendix B

The Translate Utility

Converting Spreadsheet Files

Lotus 1-2-3 for Windows includes the program TRANS.EXE, which translates .WK3 worksheet files into foreign formats and vice versa.

Import Formats Database tables or spreadsheets can be imported into 1-2-3 for Windows from any of the following formats: dBASE (.DBF), VisiCalc (.DIF), or Multiplan Release 1.2 (.SLK).

Export Formats Worksheet files can be exported to any of the following formats: dBASE (.DBF), SuperCalc 4 (.CAL), VisiCalc (.DIF), Multiplan 4.0 (.SLK), Enable 2.0 (.SSF), 1-2-3 Release 2 (.WK1), 1-2-3 Release 1A (.WKS), and Symphony (.WR1 and .WRK).

To Translate Files:

Note: The Translate Utility must have been installed during the running of Install 1-2-3. (Select **Install with Options** and select the **Translate Utility** check box.)

1. Open Windows Program Manager and select **Lotus Applications.**
2. Select **1-2-3 Translate.**
3. On the Lotus 1-2-3 Translate Utility screen, select a file format to translate in the From list box.
4. Select a file format to create in the To list box. (Move to the desired selection with the ↑ and ↓ keys, then press ↵.)
5. Information appears on the selections you've made. Press **Esc.**
6. If necessary, enter a new path, including subdirectory and file name in the Source File field. (The correct extension is mandatory.)

7. A list of source files is displayed. Highlight the desired file and press ↵.
8. If necessary, reenter the path and file name for the new file in the Target File field, and press ↵. (The correct extension is mandatory.)
   or
   Press ↵ to accept the path and file name shown.
9. If the Source and Target information is correct, select **Yes** to proceed.
   or
   Select **No** to enter new information.
10. The prompt **Translation In Progress** appears. When a new file has been created, the prompt **Translation Successful** appears.
11. Press ↵ to perform the same type of translation on another file.
    or
    Press **Esc** to select another format to translate.
12. From the file format selection screen, press **Esc**, then **Yes** to quit the program.

• **NOTES** Depending on the file types selected, the program may prompt for various selections after step 9. For example, you may be asked whether to overwrite an existing file, select all or just one worksheet from a three-dimensional file, translate @functions as add-in programs or as labels, select rowwise or columnwise orientation of .DIF files, or select named range or entire file for .DBF files.

In general, untranslatable items usually are converted to labels.

Translate will not work on 1-2-3 files created with File Extract To. You must recreate the file with File Save As.

If your system lacks sufficient memory, Translate will not run from the icon. In such cases, it will be necessary to run the program from the DOS command prompt. The procedure for doing this is described in Appendix A of the *1-2-3 for Windows User's Guide.*

Appendix C

Macro Language

Macro commands are contained in worksheet cells and have the following syntax:

{*MacroName*} with no arguments

or

{*MacroName Argument1,Argument2,..,ArgumentN*}

The macro command string, including its name and arguments, must be entirely enclosed by a set of braces {}. Optional arguments are shown in this listing in brackets [](Do not use brackets in command syntax). The following general rules apply:

- Range references can be addresses or names.
- Values, except where noted, can be numeric values, labels, formulas that generate values or labels, or range references that contain values.
- Precede a text formula with a plus sign (+).
- Literal strings must be enclosed in quotation marks " ".
- Most arguments that require string values can also be formulas that generate labels or range references that contain labels.
- With some commands, "Format" is an optional string value specifying a Clipboard format for data typing, such as BITMAP, METAFILEPICT, or TEXT. The value can be a literal string enclosed in quotation marks, or a formula or range reference that results in a string.

Clipboard Commands

Pass data to and from the Windows Clipboard, or scratch-pad memory area.

{edit-clear [*Range*][,"*Property*"]} Permanently deletes from *Range* (or current pointer location), the property specified by one of the following keywords (enclosed in quotation marks): CONTENTS, FORMATS, GRAPHS, or STYLES.

{edit-copy [*Range*][,"*Format*"]} Copies the contents of *Range* (or current pointer location) to the Clipboard, in one of the Clipboard formats.

{edit-copy-graph} Copies the contents of the current graph window to the Clipboard.

{edit-cut [*Range*][,"*Format*"]} Cuts (deletes and copies) the contents of *Range* (or current pointer location) to the Clipboard, in one of the Clipboard formats.

{edit-paste [*Range*][,"*Format*"]} Copies to *Range* (or current pointer location) in the current worksheet the contents of the Clipboard, in one of the Clipboard formats.

{edit-paste-link [*Range*]} Pastes the contents of the Clipboard to *Range* (or current pointer location) in the current worksheet, establishing a data link with the source file.

Data Manipulation Commands

Apply to worksheet data.

{appendbelow *ToRange,FromRange*} Copies the contents of *FromRange* to the rows below *ToRange.*

{appendright *ToRange,FromRange*} Copies the contents of *FromRange* to the column to the right of *ToRange.*

{blank *Range*} Fills *Range* with blanks without changing its formatting.

{contents *ToRange,FromRange*[,*N*][,*CodeNumber*]} Copies contents of *FromRange* to *ToRange* as a label of *N* (1–240) characters, according to *CodeNumber* (0–127) format.

{let *Range,Value*} Enters a numeric value or left-aligned label in the first cell of *Range.*

{put *Range,ColumnNumber,RowNumber,Value*} Enters *Value* at the specified offsets in *Range.*

{recalc ***Range [,Formula][,N]*}** Recalculates values in *Range,* subject to condition *Formula* (logical, numeric, or text), iterated *N* times. Proceeds rowwise.

{recalccol ***Range [,Formula][,N]*}** Same as **recalc,** but proceeds columnwise.

Dynamic Data Exchange (DDE) Commands

Control low-level data links to other Windows applications. (See also "Link" commands.)

{dde-advise ***MacroRange,"ItemName"[,"Format"]*}** When there is an update in the external application, triggers the *ItemName* macro in MacroRange.

{dde-close} Terminates the link and transactions with a Windows application.

{dde-execute "*ExternalCommand*"} Sends the command string *ExternalCommand* to a Windows application.

{dde-open "*ApplicationName*","*TopicName*"[,*Range*]} Opens a named Windows DDE application and links to file *TopicName.* Optionally enters a conversation identification number at *Range* in the current worksheet.

{dde-poke ***Range,"ItemName"[,"Format"]*}** Sends the contents of *Range* to the linked *ItemName* topic or file in a Windows application.

{dde-request ***Range,"ItemName"[,"Format"]*}** Receives the contents of the linked *ItemName* topic or file in a Windows application into the specified *Range.*

{dde-unadvise "*ItemName*"[,"*Format*"]} Required ending statement for a **dde-advise** subroutine.

{dde-use ***N*}** Selects the DDE conversation number *N,* using the identification number returned by **dde-open.**

External Table Control Commands

Apply only to database query transactions with SQL servers.

{commit ["*DriverName*"][,"*DatabaseName*"]} Finalizes pending transactions. Use both arguments or none (all pending transactions).

{rollback ["*DriverName*"][,"*DatabaseName*"]} Cancels pending transactions. Use both arguments or none (to cancel all pending transactions).

File Manipulation Commands

Apply to a text file, only one of which can be open at a given time.

{close} Updates and closes the text file opened previously with the **open** command.

{filesize *Range*} Counts the bytes in the currently open text file and places the result in *Range.*

{getpos *Range*} Gets the current byte-pointer position in the open text file and places it in *Range.*

{open "*Path\FileName.Extension*",*A*} Opens a file for the following access types (*A* code): A = read-write-append, M = read-modify-write, R = read-only, or W = read-write.

{read *ByteCount,Range*} In the open text file and starting at the byte-pointer position, reads *ByteCount* characters into the worksheet *Range.*

{readln *Range*} In the open text file and beginning at the byte-pointer position, reads the rest of the current line into the worksheet *Range* and advances the pointer to the next line.

{setpos *ByteNumber*} In the open text file, moves the byte pointer to the offset *ByteNumber.*

{write *String*} In the open text file and starting at the byte-pointer position, copies the string value to the file.

{writeln *String*} Same as **write,** but adds a carriage return-line feed to end the current line.

Flow-of-Control Commands

Control the execution of macros, subroutines, loops, and conditional statements.

{*subroutine* [*Argument1,Argument2,..,ArgumentN*]} Calls the named *subroutine* (preferably a range name), passing up to 31 arguments to it, and returns control to the calling macro.

{branch *Range*} Transfers control to the macro in *Range* and does not return.

{define *Range1,Range2,..,RangeN*} Specifies storage locations for arguments passed to a subroutine (typically the first statement in a subroutine).

{dispatch *Range*} Similar to **branch,** but transfers control indirectly, according to conditional statements in *Range.*

{for *CounterCell,Start,Stop,Step,SubroutineName*} Initiates a for-loop, iterating *SubroutineName,* counting from *Start* to *Stop* in increments of *Step,* and holding the count in the address *CounterCell.*

{forbreak} Prematurely terminates a for-loop initiated with **for.**

{if *ConditionFormula*} If the result of the formula is nonzero, executes the statements in the same cell.

{launch "*Path\ExternalCommand*"[,*WindowCode*]} Starts an external windows application with the *ExternalCommand* string, according to an optional window-control code 0–9.

{onerror *GoToRange*[,*MessageRange*]} On encountering a macro error, branches to the macro in *GoToRange* and displays the contents of *MessageRange.*

{quit} Immediately terminates all macro execution.

{restart} Clears the subroutine stack and terminates the macro after the end of the current subroutine.

{return} Passes control from the current subroutine back to the macro that called it.

{system "*OSCommand*"} Suspends macro processing temporarily and passes the command string to the operating system.

Interactive Commands

Permit user input.

{?} Suspends macro execution temporarily until the user presses ↵, permitting input from the keyboard.

{breakoff} Disables program termination through Ctrl-Break for the duration of a macro.

{breakon} Cancels a previous **breakoff** command.

{form *InputRange*[,*CallTableRange*][,*IncludeRange*][,*Exclude-Range*]} Suspends macro execution so that the user can fill in a form in the worksheet (at location *Range*). *CallTableRange* is a two-column range of key-to-macro equivalents. *IncludeRange* and *ExcludeRange* include keystrokes to allow and to ignore.

{formbreak} Terminates a previous **form** command.

{get *Range*} Suspends the current macro until the user presses a key and places the response (key value) as a left-aligned label in *Range.*

{getlabel "*PromptString*",*Range*} Suspends the current macro and displays *PromptString* in the 1-2-3 Classic window. Records keystrokes until the user selects OK or presses ↵. Recorded information becomes a left-aligned label in *Range.*

{getnumber "*PromptString*",*Range*} Suspends the current macro and displays *PromptString* in the 1-2-3 Classic window. Records keystrokes until the user selects OK or presses ↵, calculates the recorded information, and places the numeric result in *Range.*

{look *Range*} Gets the first character from the type-ahead buffer and places it as a left-aligned label in *Range.* If the buffer is empty, returns an apostrophe ('), or left-aligned label prefix.

{menubranch *Range*} Displays a macro menu contained in *Range* in the 1-2-3 Classic window. After the user makes a selection from the menu, branches to the corresponding macro.

{menucall *Range*} Same as **menubranch,** except executes a subroutine call instead of branching to a macro.

{wait *TimeNumber*} Suspends macro execution until the computer's clock reaches *TimeNumber,* typically a formula for calculating the interval **@now+@time(***Arguments*). (See "@time" in Part IV.)

Link Commands

Control high-level data links to other Windows applications. (See also "Dynamic Data Exchange (DDE) Commands.")

{link-assign "*LinkName*",*Range* [,"*Property1*"][,"*Property2*"][,"*Property3*"]} Assigns the *LinkName* created with **link-create** to the specified *Range,* clearing properties as indicated by the keywords: CONTENTS, FORMATS, GRAPHS, and/or STYLES.

{link-create "*LinkName*","*ApplicationName*","*TopicName*","*ItemName*"[,"*Format*"][,"*Mode*"]} Creates the link *LinkName* (1–15 characters) to an application, optionally using one of the Clipboard formats and the Mode AUTOMATIC or MANUAL (requires **link-update**) to control updating.

{link-deactivate "*LinkName*"} Severs the link *LinkName* created with **link-create** but retains the link information for later activation with **link-update**.

{link-delete "*LinkName*"} Deletes a link from the current sheet, leaving its data.

{link-remove "*LinkName*"} Removes the range being used by a DDE link, but not the link itself or its data.

{link-table *Range*} Pastes a table of DDE links to the current file in the current sheet at *Range.*

{link-update "*LinkName*"} Reactivates and/or updates the named DDE link.

Macro Key Names

Are used to reference keystrokes in macro recording and in macro command syntax.

Macro Key Name	Key Equivalent
{**down**} or {**d**}	↓
{**up**} or {**u**}	↑
{**left**} or {**l**}	←
{**right**} or {**r**}	→
{~}	~ or ↵
/ or < or {**menu**}	/ or <
{{ }	{

Macro Key Name	Key Equivalent
{}}	}
{alt} or **{menubar}** or **{mb}**	Alt
{zoom}	Alt-F6(Zoom)
{app1}	Alt-F7(App1)
{app2}	Alt-F8(App2)
{app3}	Alt-F9(App3)
{backspace} or **{bs}**	Backspace
{file}	Ctrl-End
{prevfile} or **{pf}** or **{file}{ps}**	Ctrl-End Ctrl-PgDn
{nextfile} or **{nf}** or **{file}{ns}**	Ctrl-End Ctrl-PgUp
{lastfile} or **{lf}** or **{file}{end}**	Ctrl-End Ctrl-End
{firstfile} or **{ff}** or **{file}{home}**	Ctrl-End Ctrl-Home
{firstcell} or **{fc}**	Ctrl-Home
{backtab} or **{bigleft}**	Ctrl-←
{prevsheet} or **{ps}**	Ctrl-PgDn
{nextsheet} or **{ns}**	Ctrl-PgUp
{anchor}	Ctrl-period
{bigright} or **{tab}**	Ctrl-→
{delete} or **{del}**	Del
{end}	End
{lastcell} or **{lc}**	End Ctrl-Home
{escape} or **{esc}**	Esc
{help}	F1(Help)
{edit}	F2(Edit)
{name}	F3(Name)
{anchor}	F4 in READY mode

Macro Key Name	Key Equivalent
{abs}	F4(Abs) in EDIT, POINT, or VALUE modes
{goto}	F5(Goto)
{window}	F6(Pane)
{query}	F7(Query)
{table}	F8(Table)
{calc}	F9(Calc)
{alt} or **{menubar}** or **{mb}**	F10(Menu)
{home}	Home
{insert} or **{ins}**	Ins
{pgdn}	PageDown
{pgup}	PageUp
{tab}	Tab

Screen Control Commands

Control the display device.

{beep *N*} Triggers a tone from the computer, according to the numeric code *N* (1–4).

{break} Depending on the situation, clears the line of data currently being entered, exits the current dialog box, or returns the program to READY mode.

{frameoff} Turns off display of a frame around the worksheet.

{frameon} Turns on display of a frame around the worksheet.

{graphoff} Clears the graph display triggered by **graphon.**

{graphon [*GraphName*][*,NODISPLAY*]} Displays *GraphName* while a macro runs. Without arguments, displays the current graph instead. *NODISPLAY* makes *GraphName* current but does not display it.

{indicate *String*} Displays *String* as the mode indicator on the 1-2-3 program screen.

{paneloff [CLEAR]} Freezes and optionally clears the control panel and status line of 1-2-3 until a **panelon** command.

{panelon} Unfreezes a display locked by **paneloff.**

{windowsoff} Prevents updates to the screen while a macro is being executed.

{windowson} Cancels **windowsoff.**

Window Control Commands

Control the Windows environment.

{app-adjust *XPixel,YPixel,Width,Height*} Places the 1-2-3 program window *X* pixels from the left and *Y* pixels from the top of the screen and sizes it to *Width* by *Height* pixels.

{app-state ["*State*"]} Controls the application window according to one of the following string constants (*State*): MAXIMIZE, MINIMIZE, or RESTORE.

{window-adjust *XPixel,YPixel,Width,Height*} Places the current window *X* pixels from the left and *Y* pixels from the top of the screen and sizes it to *Width* by *Height* pixels.

{window-select "*WindowName*"} Makes *WindowName* the current, or active, window.

{window-state ["*State*"]} Controls the active window according to one of the following string constants (*State*): MAXIMIZE, MINIMIZE, or RESTORE.

Appendix D

Adobe Type Manager

At the conclusion of the Install 1-2-3 program, you are asked whether you wish to install Adobe Type Manager (ATM). This Windows application has several uses with Lotus 1-2-3, including:

- Improves the quality of displayed fonts and outputs to dot-matrix, ink-jet, or laser printers.
- Enables printing of PostScript fonts on printers that don't otherwise support them.
- Permits you to load additional software fonts that are compatible with PostScript Type 1 format.
- Works with any Windows application that supports these fonts.
- Once installed, operates without further intervention from the user.

To Install ATM:

1. Be sure no other font manager resides in memory.
2. Select and install printers in Windows.
3. Insert the ATM Program Disk in drive A.
4. Start Windows Program Manager.
5. Select **File** then **Run.**
6. Enter **a:\install** in the Command Line text box.
7. Select **OK.**
8. If necessary, enter new path information for fonts and font metrics files in the ATM Installer dialog box and select **Install.**
9. Select **OK.**

10. Before ATM can become active, you must exit to DOS and restart Windows.

To Control ATM:

1. Start Windows Program Manager.
2. Select the **Main** program group.
3. Select **ATM Control Panel.**
4. To make ATM inactive, select **ATM Off.**
5. To unload a font from the current set, select the font from the Installed ATM Fonts list box, then **Remove** and **Yes** to confirm the removal.
6. To adjust the size of the Font Cache, click on the ↑ or ↓ buttons.
7. To use bitmap fonts that reside in a printer, select the check box **Use Pre-built or Resident Bitmap Fonts.**
8. Select **Exit.**

To Add Fonts:

1. Perform steps 1–4 of "To Control ATM."
2. Select **Add.**
3. If necessary, enter new path information in the Target Directory text boxes.
4. Make selections from the Directories (including device letters) and Available Fonts list boxes in the Add ATM Fonts dialog box.
5. If necessary, insert font distribution disks.
6. Select **Add.**
7. Select **Exit.**
8. Exit to DOS and restart Windows.

• **NOTES** ATM requires 250K of disk space, plus 40K for each font. The program is always active in any Windows application that supports PostScript Type 1 fonts unless you explicitly turn it off through the ATM Control Panel.

PostScript outline fonts have file extensions .PFB. Metric fonts are .PFM files.

The default size of the font cache in system memory is 96K. Increase the size of the cache if performance seems slow. Valid settings are 64K–8192K. You want the lowest number that achieves acceptable performance.

Using bitmap fonts can improve system performance with intelligent printers, offloading font calculations from the CPU. Pre-built fonts are held in software on the system disk and downloaded to the printer. (PCL fonts used with printers such as the HP LaserJet series are stored in the subdirectory \PCLFONTS.) Resident fonts are in cartridges that are inserted into the printer.

Index

A

B

C

D

E

F

G

H

I

M

N

O

P

Q

R

S

U

V

W

X

Y

Z

Function Keys

Key	Description
Alt-F1 (Compose)	Make custom key assignments
Alt-F2 (Step)	Toggle macro STEP mode
Alt-F3 (Run)	Display list of executable macros
Alt-F6 (Zoom)	Enlarge/shrink current window
Alt-F7 (Add-In 1)	Start Add-in program #1
Alt-F8 (Add-In 2)	Start Add-in program #2
Alt-F9 (Add-In 3)	Start Add-in program #3
F1 (Help)	Access Help system
F2 (Edit)	In EDIT mode, edit cell entries
F3 (Name)	Select from list of names for current command or formula
F4 in READY mode	Anchor cell pointer
F4 (Abs) in EDIT, POINT, or VALUE modes	Change reference from relative to absolute or absolute to mixed
F5 (Goto)	Move pointer to specified cell or range
F6 (Pane)	Move pointer to another pane created with Window Split
F7 (Query)	Perform most recent Data Query Extract or Find; switch between FIND and READY modes
F8 (Table)	Repeat last Data What-if Table command
F9 (Calc)	Force worksheet recalculation and file update
F10 (Menu)	Activate the menu bar

Accelerator Keys

Key	1-2-3 Command Equivalent
Alt-backspace	Edit Undo
Alt-F4	File Exit
Ctrl-Ins	Edit Copy
Ctrl-*letter*	Tools Macro Run
Del	Edit Clear
Shift-Del	Edit Cut
Shift-Ins	Edit Paste